MW00929286

Yucatán

Travel guide 2025

Exploring the Wonders of Mexico's Hidden
Gem

David E. Welter

Copyright © 2025 by [David E. Welter]

All rights reserved. No part of this publication may be reproduced, distributed, or transmitted in any form or by any means, including photocopying, recording, or other electronic or mechanical methods, without the prior written permission of the publisher, except in the case of brief quotations embodied in critical reviews and certain other non-commercial uses permitted by copyright law.

INTRODUCTION

Ah, the Yucatán Peninsula—a place where the ordinary world feels a million miles away. Imagine this: It's dawn, the sun peeks over the horizon, casting a warm golden glow over the lush green landscape. You're standing at the edge of the world, or so it feels, with a cup of hot coffee in your hand, listening to the symphony of birds and the gentle rustling of the jungle.

The Yucatán isn't just a place to visit; it's a place to experience. The adventure begins the moment you set foot in this enchanting land. My journey started in the vibrant city of Mérida, the capital of Yucatán. Mérida, with its colonial architecture and bustling markets, feels like a step back in time. The streets are alive with the sounds of daily life—vendors calling out their wares, the clattering of horse-drawn carriages, and the hum of conversations in Spanish and Maya.

One of the highlights of my trip was visiting the ancient Mayan ruins of Chichén Itzá. There's something awe-inspiring about standing before the iconic El Castillo pyramid, knowing it was built over a thousand years ago. The pyramid, with its precise astronomical alignments, is a testament to the advanced knowledge of the Mayan civilization. As I wandered through the ruins, I could almost hear the whispers of the past, telling stories of a once-great city that thrived in the heart of the jungle.

But the Yucatán isn't just about its rich history. It's also a place of natural wonders. One of the most magical experiences was swimming in a cenote. These natural sinkholes, filled with crystal-clear water, are scattered throughout the region. Each cenote has its own unique character—some are open to the sky, others hidden in underground caves. I remember the feeling of diving into the cool, refreshing water, surrounded by the sound of dripping water and the echo of my own breath. It was like being in another world, far removed from the hustle and bustle of everyday life.

Of course, no trip to the Yucatán would be complete without indulging in the local cuisine. From the hearty cochinita pibil, a slow-roasted pork dish marinated in citrus and spices, to the refreshing taste of a freshly made margarita, every meal was a delight for the senses. I spent hours exploring the local markets, sampling exotic fruits, and chatting with vendors about their recipes and culinary traditions. The food in the Yucatán is more than just nourishment; it's a reflection of the region's rich cultural heritage.

One of my favorite memories was a visit to the coastal town of Tulum. The white sandy beaches, turquoise waters, and ancient Mayan ruins perched on cliffs overlooking the sea made for a picture-perfect setting. I spent my days lounging on the beach, snorkeling in the coral reefs, and exploring the ruins. At night, the town came alive with music, laughter, and the scent of freshly grilled seafood wafting through the air. It was here, under the starry sky, that I truly felt the magic of the Yucatán.

The Yucatán Peninsula is also home to a vibrant and diverse community. The people I met during my travels were warm, welcoming, and eager to share their stories. From the friendly locals who offered me directions and advice to the passionate guides who brought the history and culture of the region to life, every encounter added a new layer to my experience. Their pride in their heritage and their love for their homeland were palpable, and it was impossible not to be swept up in their enthusiasm.

As my journey through the Yucatán came to an end, I found myself reflecting on the memories I had made. The Yucatán is a place of contrasts—ancient and modern, wild and civilized, serene and lively. It's a place where history is written in the stones and the jungle whispers secrets of the past. But more than that, it's a place that invites you to slow down, to savor each moment, and to connect with the world around you.

In the end, my time in the Yucatán was more than just a vacation; it was a journey of discovery, both of the world and of myself. It's a place that leaves an indelible mark on your soul, a place that beckons you to return, time and time again. And as the memories of my adventure fade into the background of daily life, I know that a part of me will always be wandering those ancient ruins, swimming in those crystal-clear cenotes, and lounging on those sun-kissed beaches. The Yucatán is a place that stays with you, long after you've left its shores, and I feel incredibly lucky to have experienced its magic.

So, if you're ever looking for a destination that offers a rich tapestry of history, culture, and natural beauty, look no further than the Yucatán Peninsula. Whether you're an adventurer, a history buff, a foodie, or simply someone looking to unwind, the Yucatán has something for everyone. And who knows? You might just find yourself falling in love with this enchanting corner of the world, just like I did.

Historical Background

The Yucatán Peninsula is like a living museum, where history is woven into every aspect of life. My journey there was more than just a trip; it was a step back in time to witness the legacy of ancient civilizations, meet the descendants of the Maya, and experience a culture that has been shaped by centuries of conquest, colonization, and resilience.

My adventure began in Mérida, a city that pulses with both modern energy and old-world charm. The cobblestone streets and grand colonial buildings tell stories of Spanish conquests, while the bustling markets and lively festivals celebrate a vibrant present. Here, history isn't confined to museums; it's in the rhythm of daily life, from the traditional dances performed in the town squares to the ancient rituals still observed by the local people.

One of the most unforgettable experiences was visiting Chichén Itzá, a UNESCO World Heritage site and one of the New Seven Wonders of the World. Walking through this ancient city, I could almost hear the echoes of the past. The massive El Castillo pyramid, which dominates the site, is not just an architectural marvel but also a testament to the astronomical prowess of the Mayans. Every detail, from the number of steps to the precise alignment with celestial bodies, reflects a deep understanding of the cosmos.

As I explored further, I stumbled upon the Great Ball Court, where the Maya played their ceremonial game, which was as much a religious ritual as it was a sport. The walls of the court still bear the carvings of players and the rituals that accompanied these games. It's said that the outcome of the games could be a matter of life and death, adding a sense of solemnity to the site.

But Yucatán's history isn't all about the grand and the ancient. It's also found in the simple, everyday moments. Like the time I visited a traditional Mayan village and sat down to a meal prepared by a local family. The food, cooked over an open fire, was a revelation. The flavors of cochinita pibil, a slow-roasted pork marinated in citrus and spices, and the handmade tortillas, were a testament to culinary traditions passed down through generations.

The Yucatán is also famous for its cenotes, natural sinkholes that were sacred to the Maya. Swimming in the cool, clear waters of a cenote, surrounded by the lush jungle, was like being in another world. These cenotes were not just sources of fresh water, but also sites for rituals and offerings. As I floated in the tranquil water, I felt a deep connection to the past, to the people who had come to these waters for centuries seeking purification and renewal.

Tulum was another highlight of my journey. This coastal town, with its stunning beaches and cliff-top ruins, is a place where history and natural beauty coexist. The ancient ruins of Tulum, once a major port for the Mayan civilization, stand sentinel over the turquoise waters of the Caribbean. Walking among these ruins at sunrise, with the waves crashing below, was an experience that felt almost otherworldly.

In every corner of the Yucatán, history is alive and waiting to be discovered. From the grandiose ruins of ancient cities to the small, everyday moments that reveal the resilience and continuity of Mayan culture, the peninsula is a place where the past is not just remembered but lived. It's a place that invites you to slow down, to listen to the stories of the land and its people, and to find your own connection to the rich tapestry of history that makes the Yucatán so unique.

So, if you're looking for a destination where history isn't just something to learn about but something to experience, the Yucatán Peninsula should be at the top of your list. Whether you're exploring ancient ruins, swimming in sacred cenotes, or simply enjoying a meal with locals, you'll find that the history of this region is not just in its past but in every moment of the present.

Climate and Best Times to Visit

The Yucatán Peninsula enjoys a tropical climate, which means it's warm and sunny for most of the year. However, there are a few things to keep in mind when planning your visit.

First off, the region has a distinct rainy season from June to October, when the weather can be hot and humid with frequent downpours. Temperatures during this time can soar above 35°C (95°F), making outdoor activities quite challenging. On the flip side, the dry season from November to May offers more pleasant weather, with daytime temperatures ranging from 25°C to 30°C (77°F to 86°F).

If you're looking to avoid the crowds and enjoy milder weather, November and early March are ideal. During these months, the weather is comfortably warm, and you'll find fewer tourists compared to the peak season from December to April. Keep in mind that prices for accommodation and flights can be higher during the high season, so booking in advance is recommended.

It's also worth noting that the Yucatán Peninsula experiences hurricane season from June to November, with the most intense activity typically occurring in August and September. While hurricanes are relatively rare, it's a good idea to stay informed about weather conditions if you're traveling during this period.

Overall, the best time to visit the Yucatán Peninsula depends on your preferences for weather and crowd levels. Whether you're looking to soak up the sun on the beaches or explore ancient ruins, there's a time of year that's perfect for your adventure.

Cultural Significance

The Yucatán Peninsula holds a unique cultural significance that's deeply rooted in its ancient history and diverse heritage. It's a place where the past and present seamlessly blend, creating a rich tapestry of traditions, customs, and artistic expressions.

One of the most striking aspects of Yucatán's cultural heritage is its connection to the ancient Maya civilization. The region is dotted with impressive archaeological sites like Chichén Itzá, Uxmal, and Tulum, each offering a glimpse into the lives of the Maya people. These ancient cities were centers of political, economic, and religious activity, and their ruins continue to be a source of fascination and pride for the local population.

The Maya people have left an indelible mark on the Yucatán, not just through their architecture and art, but also through their language and traditions. Many communities still speak Yucatec Maya, preserving a linguistic heritage that dates back thousands of years. Festivals and ceremonies, such as the Day of the Dead (Hanal Pixán) and the traditional ball game (Pok ta Pok), are celebrated with great enthusiasm, showcasing the enduring influence of Maya culture.

Colonial history also plays a significant role in the cultural landscape of the Yucatán Peninsula. The arrival of Spanish conquistadors in the 16th century brought about profound changes, blending European and indigenous elements. This fusion is evident in the region's architecture, cuisine, and religious practices. Colonial cities like Mérida and Valladolid are home to beautiful churches, plazas, and mansions that reflect this unique blend of cultures.

The Yucatán Peninsula is also known for its vibrant arts scene. From traditional crafts like hammocks and pottery to contemporary art galleries and music festivals, there's no shortage of creative expression. The region's music is particularly noteworthy, with genres like Trova Yucateca and Jarana Yucateca that blend indigenous rhythms with Spanish influences. These musical styles are often performed at local festivals, providing a lively soundtrack to the region's cultural celebrations.

Cuisine is another essential aspect of Yucatán's cultural significance. The food here is a delicious blend of Maya, Spanish, and Caribbean influences. Dishes like cochinita pibil, papadzules, and panuchos are staples of Yucatecan cuisine, each with its unique flavors and ingredients. Food is not just sustenance here; it's an integral part of social and cultural life, with recipes often passed down through generations.

The cultural significance of the Yucatán Peninsula is also reflected in its vibrant festivals and events. From the colorful Carnaval celebrations to the solemn processions of Semana Santa (Holy Week), these events are a testament to the region's rich cultural heritage. They provide an opportunity for locals and visitors alike to experience the traditions, music, dance, and cuisine that make the Yucatán so unique.

In essence, the Yucatán Peninsula is a place where history, tradition, and modernity coexist. Its cultural significance lies in its ability to preserve ancient customs while embracing contemporary influences. Whether you're exploring ancient ruins, participating in a traditional festival, or simply enjoying a meal with locals, the Yucatán offers a deeply immersive cultural experience that leaves a lasting impression.

1 WEEK ITINERARY

Here's a one-week itinerary for the Yucatán Peninsula that balances historical exploration, natural beauty, and cultural immersion:

Day 1: Arrival in Mérida
- Morning: Arrive in Mérida, the capital of Yucatán. Settle into your accommodation and take a stroll around the city center.
- Afternoon: Visit the Cathedral of San Ildefonso and the Plaza Grande.
- Evening: Enjoy a traditional Yucatecan meal at a local restaurant.

Day 2: Mérida and Surroundings
- Morning: Explore the Gran Museo del Mundo Maya.
- Afternoon: Visit the Hacienda Yaxcopoil for a glimpse into the region's colonial history.
- Evening: Relax at the Parque de la Mejor Vida.

Day 3: Chichén Itzá

- Morning: Take a day trip to Chichén Itzá, one of the New Seven Wonders of the World.

- Afternoon: Explore the ancient ruins and learn about the Mayan civilization.

- Evening: Return to Mérida and enjoy a leisurely evening.

Day 4: Valladolid

- Morning: Drive to Valladolid and visit the Convent of San Bernardino de Siena.

- Afternoon: Explore the town's charming streets and visit the Cenote Zaci.

- Evening: Dine at a local restaurant and experience Valladolid's nightlife.

Day 5: Ek Balam

- Morning: Take a short drive to the ancient Mayan city of Ek Balam.

- Afternoon: Wander through the ruins and enjoy the peaceful surroundings.

- Evening: Return to Valladolid and relax.

Day 6: Tulum

- Morning: Drive to Tulum and visit the archaeological site overlooking the Caribbean Sea.
- Afternoon: Spend time on the beautiful beaches and explore the town.
- Evening: Enjoy a sunset dinner at a beachfront restaurant.

Day 7: Cenotes and Departure

- Morning: Visit the Cenote Dos Ojos for a refreshing swim.
- Afternoon: Explore the Cenote Calavera and enjoy the natural beauty.
- Evening: Return to Mérida for your departure.

Getting There And Around

Major Airports

Arriving in the Yucatán Peninsula is a breeze, thanks to several major airports that cater to international and domestic travelers alike. Each airport offers a gateway to the region's rich culture, history, and natural beauty, setting the stage for an unforgettable adventure.

The primary entry point for most visitors is the Cancún International Airport (CUN), one of the busiest airports in Mexico. Located just outside the city of Cancún, this airport is a major hub for international flights from North America, Europe, and beyond. Its modern facilities and wide range of services make it a convenient choice for travelers. Upon landing, you'll find yourself just a short drive away from the pristine beaches of Cancún and the Riviera Maya, as well as the ancient ruins of Tulum and Chichén Itzá.

Another important airport is the Mérida International Airport (MID), also known as Manuel Crescencio Rejón International Airport. Situated in the capital city of Yucatán, Mérida Airport serves as a key gateway to the region's historical and cultural attractions. Flights from the United States, Canada, and other parts of Mexico regularly land here. The airport is relatively small but efficient, providing easy access to Mérida's colonial architecture, vibrant markets, and nearby archaeological sites.

Chetumal International Airport (CTM) is another option for travelers heading to the southern part of the Yucatán Peninsula. Located in the capital of the state of Quintana Roo, this airport connects travelers with the lesser-explored areas of the region, including the coastal town of Bacalar, famous for its stunning Lagoon of Seven Colors. Chetumal Airport is smaller than Cancún and Mérida, but it offers a more relaxed travel experience and serves as a convenient starting point for adventures in southern Yucatán and Belize.

For those planning to explore the island of Cozumel, the Cozumel International Airport (CZM) is the gateway. This airport caters primarily to tourists visiting the island's renowned dive sites and luxury resorts. Direct flights from the United States and Canada make it easy to reach this tropical paradise. The airport's proximity to Cozumel's main town means you can quickly transition from your flight to relaxing on the beach or embarking on a snorkeling adventure.

Lastly, there is the Playa del Carmen Airport (PCM), a smaller airport mainly serving private and charter flights. While not as busy as the other airports, it provides a convenient option for those looking to stay in Playa del Carmen or the nearby resorts. The airport is close to the town center, allowing for a swift transfer to your accommodation.

Each of these airports provides a unique entry point to the Yucatán Peninsula, ensuring that no matter where you land, you'll be ready to dive into the region's rich offerings. Whether you're here for the ancient ruins, the vibrant culture, or the stunning natural landscapes, the journey begins the moment you touch down.

Public Transportation

Getting around the Yucatán Peninsula is an adventure in itself. Public transportation here offers a mix of modern convenience and local charm, making it an integral part of your travel experience.

Buses are the backbone of public transport in the Yucatán. ADO, the largest bus company, operates a network of comfortable, air-conditioned coaches connecting major cities and tourist destinations. Whether you're traveling from Cancún to Mérida or heading to smaller towns like Valladolid or Bacalar, you'll find ADO buses reliable and reasonably priced. The terminals are bustling hubs of activity, with vendors selling snacks and locals waiting for their rides.

For shorter distances, colectivos are the way to go. These shared minibuses or vans zip between towns and popular sites. Hailing a colectivo is straightforward—they usually wait at designated stops or roam the main streets looking for passengers. They're an affordable and efficient way to get around, and riding with locals can give you a more authentic glimpse into daily life.

If you're planning to explore the coast, ferries are essential, especially for visiting islands like Cozumel and Isla Mujeres. Regular ferry services operate from Playa del Carmen and Cancún, offering a scenic and leisurely way to reach these tropical paradises. The journey across the turquoise waters is an experience in itself, with the sea breeze and stunning views setting the perfect tone for your island adventures.

Taxis are readily available in cities and tourist areas. In Mérida, Cancún, and Playa del Carmen, you can easily flag one down on the street or find them at taxi stands. It's always a good idea to confirm the fare before starting your journey, as meters aren't always used. Taxis offer flexibility and convenience, especially if you're traveling with luggage or heading to less accessible locations.

For those who prefer a bit more independence, renting a car is a popular option. The Yucatán's roads are generally well-maintained, and having your own vehicle gives you the freedom to explore at your own pace. Whether you're driving through the jungle to reach remote cenotes or taking a coastal route to hidden beaches, a car lets you chart your own course. Just remember to carry your driver's license, and be mindful of local driving customs.

Cycling enthusiasts will find the Yucatán to be a bike-friendly region. In cities like Mérida and Valladolid, bike rentals are available, and dedicated bike paths make exploring easy and enjoyable. Pedaling through historic streets, past colonial buildings, and vibrant markets allows for a slow-paced, immersive experience.

Navigating public transportation in the Yucatán Peninsula is more than just getting from point A to point B. It's an opportunity to interact with locals, soak in the scenery, and experience the region's unique rhythm. Whether you're boarding a bus, hopping on a colectivo, or renting a bike, every journey becomes a part of your adventure, adding depth and character to your Yucatán experience.

Renting a car

Renting a car in the Yucatán Peninsula can greatly enhance your travel experience, giving you the freedom to explore at your own pace and venture off the beaten path. The process is straightforward, but there are a few tips and things to keep in mind to ensure a smooth journey.

First, booking your car in advance is always a good idea, especially during the high tourist season from December to April. Many international car rental companies operate in the region, including Hertz, Avis, and Budget, alongside local agencies. You can pick up your rental car at major airports like

Cancún International Airport, Mérida International Airport, and even smaller airports like Chetumal.

When it comes to vehicle choice, consider the type of travel you'll be doing. If you're planning to stick to major cities and highways, a compact car might be sufficient. However, if you plan to explore rural areas, visit remote cenotes, or drive through jungle roads, an SUV or a vehicle with good ground clearance might be more suitable.

Insurance is a key aspect of renting a car in the Yucatán. Basic insurance is typically included in the rental fee, but it's highly recommended to opt for additional coverage to avoid hefty out-of-pocket expenses in case of an accident. Collision Damage Waiver (CDW) and Liability Insurance are commonly offered. Make sure to thoroughly read the terms and conditions and understand what is covered.

Driving in the Yucatán is generally safe and the roads are well-maintained, but it's important to stay vigilant. Speed limits are posted in kilometers per hour, and it's crucial to adhere to them, especially since speed bumps (topes) are common and can appear unexpectedly, even on highways. These bumps are designed to slow down traffic in populated areas and near schools, so keep an eye out.

Parking in cities like Mérida, Cancún, and Playa del Carmen can be tricky, especially in the historic districts where streets are narrow. Look for designated parking areas or lots, and avoid parking on yellow-painted curbs which indicate no-parking zones. In some areas, you might find parking attendants who will guide you to a spot for a small fee.

Fueling up is straightforward, with plenty of gas stations along major routes. It's worth noting that gas stations in Mexico are usually full-service, so an attendant will pump the gas for you. Tipping a small amount, around 10 pesos, is appreciated.

While GPS and map apps on your smartphone can be very helpful, having a physical map as a backup is also a good idea, especially in areas with limited cell service. Familiarize yourself with the main routes and landmarks to avoid getting lost.

Lastly, it's always wise to keep essential documents handy. Carry your driver's license, passport, rental agreement, and insurance papers at all times. In case you encounter a police checkpoint, which are fairly common, you'll need to present these documents.

Renting a car opens up a world of possibilities in the Yucatán Peninsula. Whether you're planning to explore ancient Mayan ruins, take a scenic drive along the coast, or discover hidden cenotes, having your own set of wheels allows you to make the most of your adventure. Just remember to drive safely, respect local traffic laws, and enjoy the journey!

Navigating Local Roads

Driving through the Yucatán Peninsula offers a unique opportunity to explore its diverse landscapes at your own pace.

However, navigating local roads can be an adventure in itself, requiring a bit of preparation and a sense of curiosity.

First, let's talk about the main highways. The Yucatán Peninsula has a fairly modern road network, with well-maintained highways connecting major cities and tourist destinations. The primary route you'll likely encounter is Highway 180, which stretches from Cancún through Mérida and onward to Campeche. This highway is mostly a smooth ride, but it's worth noting that toll roads (called "cuotas") are common. These toll roads are usually in excellent condition and offer a quicker, more direct route, though you'll need some cash on hand to pay the tolls.

If you're traveling between smaller towns or heading to remote attractions, you'll likely find yourself on secondary roads. These roads can be narrower and occasionally less well-maintained, with the occasional pothole to watch out for. One particular aspect to be aware of is the presence of speed bumps, known locally as "topes." These speed bumps can appear suddenly, even on highways, and are meant to slow down traffic near towns and schools. They can be quite high and are usually marked with signs, but it's always a good idea to stay alert.

Navigating through towns and cities can be a bit more challenging. In places like Mérida, the layout is a grid system, which makes it relatively easy to find your way around. However, narrow streets, one-way systems, and pedestrian zones can complicate things. Using a GPS or map app is highly recommended, but don't be surprised if you occasionally need to double-check directions with locals. They are usually more than happy to help, and it's a great way to practice your Spanish!

Parking in urban areas can be tricky, especially in the historic centers where space is limited. Look for designated parking areas or lots, and be mindful of "no parking" zones, often marked by yellow curbs. In some areas, you might encounter parking attendants who will help guide you to a spot for a small tip. When parking on the street, make sure you're not blocking driveways or entrances, as this can result in fines or towing.

Fueling up is an essential part of any road trip. Gas stations are plentiful along major highways and in larger towns, but they can be scarcer in remote areas. It's a good idea to fill up whenever you have the chance, especially if you're venturing off the beaten path. Gas stations in Mexico are typically full-service, meaning an attendant will pump the gas for you. It's customary to give a small tip, around 10 pesos, for their assistance.

While driving, always carry essential documents with you. This includes your driver's license, passport, rental agreement, and insurance papers. Police checkpoints are fairly common, especially on highways, and you'll need to present these documents if asked. The checkpoints are generally routine, but it's important to remain calm and courteous.

One of the joys of driving in the Yucatán is the ability to discover hidden gems along the way. Whether it's a secluded beach, an off-the-beaten-path cenote, or a charming village, having your own vehicle allows you to explore beyond the typical tourist spots. Just remember to drive safely, respect local traffic laws, and be prepared for the occasional surprise, like livestock crossing the road or a spontaneous fiesta in a small town.

In summary, navigating local roads in the Yucatán Peninsula can be a rewarding experience, filled with unexpected discoveries and a deeper connection to the region. With a bit of preparation and a spirit of adventure, you'll find that the journey is just as memorable as the destination.

Travel Tips and Safety

Traveling through the Yucatán Peninsula is a fantastic adventure, and while the region is generally safe and welcoming, a few travel tips can enhance your experience and help you stay out of trouble.

First and foremost, it's wise to stay informed about your destination. Researching the areas you plan to visit gives you a good sense of what to expect. Familiarize yourself with local customs and traditions. The Yucatán has a rich cultural heritage, and respecting local etiquette goes a long way. For example, when visiting religious sites like churches or Mayan ruins, dress modestly and behave respectfully.

Before you set off, make sure you have all the necessary travel documents. Carry copies of your passport, driver's license, and other important papers. Keep the originals in a secure place, such as a hotel safe, and have digital copies stored online or on your device. It's also a good idea to register with your country's embassy or consulate upon arrival, just in case you need assistance during your stay.

When it comes to health and safety, there are a few key things to keep in mind. Stay hydrated, especially if you're visiting during the hot summer months. The sun can be intense, so wear sunscreen, sunglasses, and a hat to protect yourself from sunburn. Insect repellent is essential, particularly if you're exploring jungle areas or cenotes. Mosquitoes can be pesky, and some areas might have a risk of mosquito-borne illnesses.

Petty crime, like pickpocketing, can occur in touristy areas, so it's best to stay vigilant. Use a money belt or a secure bag to keep your valuables safe. Avoid flashing large amounts of cash and keep an eye on your belongings at all times. If you're carrying a backpack, wear it on the front in crowded places. Also, be cautious when using ATMs; choose machines located in well-lit, busy areas, preferably inside banks or shopping centers.

Getting around the Yucatán is relatively straightforward, but it's always good to have a plan. If you're renting a car, familiarize yourself with local traffic laws and road conditions. Be cautious of speed bumps (topes) and livestock that might wander onto the road. If you prefer public transportation, buses and colectivos are generally safe and reliable. Just make sure to have small change for fares and be aware of your surroundings

Taxis are another common mode of transportation. Always use registered taxis, and if possible, have your hotel call one for you. Agree on the fare before starting your journey, as meters aren't always used. For a more secure option, consider using ride-sharing apps available in the region.

When it comes to food and drink, the local cuisine is a highlight of any trip to the Yucatán. To avoid any digestive issues, stick to bottled water and avoid ice unless you're sure it's made from purified water. Enjoy the street food, but opt for stalls that are busy with locals, as high turnover usually means fresher food. Trying dishes like cochinita pibil and ceviche is a must, but remember to pace yourself if you're not used to spicy food.

Lastly, always trust your instincts. If something doesn't feel right, it's okay to change your plans. Whether it's avoiding a poorly lit street at night or choosing a different restaurant, your safety and comfort should always come first. The locals are generally friendly and helpful, so don't hesitate to ask for directions or advice.

Traveling in the Yucatán Peninsula offers countless opportunities for adventure and discovery. By staying informed, respecting local customs, and taking a few sensible precautions, you'll ensure that your trip is not only memorable but also safe and enjoyable. Happy travels!

Mayan Archaeological Sites

Chichen Itza

Chichén Itzá is a place where history breathes through every stone and structure, and visiting this ancient Mayan city is like stepping into a living chronicle of a lost civilization. As you approach the site, the first thing that strikes you is the towering presence of El Castillo, also known as the Temple of Kukulcán. This massive pyramid dominates the landscape, its symmetry and sheer scale leaving you in awe.

El Castillo is not just an architectural marvel but a testament to the Maya's astronomical prowess. Twice a year, during the spring and autumn equinoxes, a play of light and shadow creates the illusion of a serpent slithering down the steps of the pyramid. This phenomenon attracts visitors from around the world, eager to witness this blend of art and science in action.

Wandering through the grounds of Chichén Itzá, you encounter the Great Ball Court, the largest of its kind in Mesoamerica.

Here, the Maya played the Mesoamerican ballgame, a sport with ritualistic and possibly even sacrificial elements. The court's acoustics are astonishing; a whisper from one end can be heard clearly at the other, a feature that might have amplified the drama of the games played here.

The site is dotted with other significant structures, each with its own story. The Temple of the Warriors, with its forest of columns, hints at the military might of the ancient Maya. Nearby, the sacred Cenote Sagrado, a large natural sinkhole, served as a site for offerings and sacrifices to the gods. It's said that countless treasures, including jade, gold, and even human remains, have been recovered from its depths.

One of the most fascinating areas is the El Caracol, or the Observatory. This cylindrical building's windows are aligned with the movements of Venus, illustrating the Maya's sophisticated understanding of celestial bodies. It's humbling to think about the knowledge and skill that went into creating these alignments, considering the time period.

Chichén Itzá isn't just about monumental architecture; it's also a place where you can feel the pulse of a vibrant, complex society that once thrived here. The site was a major political, economic, and religious center during its peak, and walking through its plazas and pathways, you can almost hear the bustle of daily life from centuries past.

Exploring Chichén Itzá, you can't help but reflect on the ingenuity and resilience of the Maya civilization. They built an empire in the heart of the jungle, with advancements in writing, mathematics, and astronomy that were ahead of their time. Each structure at Chichén Itzá tells a part of this story, from the grandeur of El Castillo to the mysterious Cenote Sagrado.

Visiting Chichén Itzá is more than just a sightseeing trip; it's a journey into the heart of an ancient world, a place where past and present merge. Whether you're an avid historian, a casual traveler, or someone seeking a deeper connection to the past,

Chichén Itzá offers a profound and enriching experience that stays with you long after you've left its ancient stones behind.

Uxmal

Uxmal is a gem of the Yucatán Peninsula, shrouded in mystery and boasting a grandeur that rivals even the more famous ruins of Chichén Itzá. Visiting Uxmal feels like stepping back in time to a city that once flourished in the heart of the jungle. As you approach, the first sight that greets you is the imposing Pyramid of the Magician, or Pyramid of the Dwarf, as it's also known. This towering structure, with its rounded sides and steep steps, stands out for its unique architectural style and the legends that surround its construction.

According to Mayan folklore, the pyramid was built overnight by a dwarf with magical powers, adding an air of mystique to the site. The pyramid's design, unlike the typical stepped pyramids of the region, features rounded corners and an elliptical base, showcasing the ingenuity and creativity of the Mayan architects. Climbing to the top, you're rewarded with panoramic views of the surrounding jungle and the rest of the ruins, a breathtaking sight that brings to life the might of the ancient city.

The Nunnery Quadrangle, just a short walk from the pyramid, is another highlight. This complex of four palaces is adorned with intricate carvings and motifs that reflect the Mayan fascination with celestial bodies and deities. The carvings of snakes, jaguars, and other mythical creatures tell stories of creation, power, and the gods worshipped by the Maya. Walking through the quadrangle, you can't help but marvel at the artistry and precision of the stonework, which has stood the test of time.

One of the most striking features of Uxmal is the Governor's Palace. This long, low building sits atop a large platform and is decorated with an elaborate frieze that stretches the entire length of the structure. The detailed carvings depict scenes of Mayan mythology and daily life, with images of serpents, gods, and rulers. The palace was likely a center of administration and ceremonial activities, reflecting the political importance of Uxmal in its heyday.

Nearby, the Great Pyramid offers another impressive climb. Although not as tall as the Pyramid of the Magician, it provides an equally stunning view of the site and its surroundings. From the top, you can see the layout of the city, with its temples, plazas, and residential areas, giving you a sense of the scale and complexity of this ancient metropolis.

The House of the Turtles, named for the turtle carvings that adorn its cornice, is another fascinating structure. Turtles were associated with the rain god in Mayan culture, and their presence here suggests the importance of water and agriculture to the people of Uxmal. The building's design is simpler than some of the other structures, but its elegance and symbolism are no less impressive.

Visiting Uxmal is not just about the grand structures and impressive ruins; it's also about the atmosphere. The site is less crowded than Chichén Itzá, allowing for a more tranquil and contemplative experience. The sounds of the jungle, with birds calling and leaves rustling, provide a natural soundtrack to your exploration. The paths between the ruins are shaded by trees, offering respite from the tropical sun and creating a peaceful environment for reflection.

Uxmal's significance extends beyond its physical structures. It represents the ingenuity, artistry, and spiritual depth of the Maya civilization. The city's layout and architecture reflect a deep understanding of astronomy, religion, and social organization, offering insights into a culture that was both advanced and profoundly connected to its environment.

Spending time in Uxmal allows you to connect with a past that feels both distant and immediate. The stones and carvings may be ancient, but they resonate with the lives of the people who built and inhabited this remarkable city. It's a place where history is not just observed but felt, where the past comes alive in the present. Whether you're a history buff, an architecture enthusiast, or simply a curious traveler, Uxmal offers an experience that is both enriching and unforgettable.

Coba

Coba, tucked away in the dense jungles of the Yucatán Peninsula, is a captivating archaeological site that offers a fascinating glimpse into the ancient Maya civilization. Unlike the more polished and well-trodden paths of Chichén Itzá, Coba retains an air of mystery and raw beauty, inviting visitors to step into a world where history and nature intertwine seamlessly.

Driving through the lush landscape to reach Coba, you can't help but feel a sense of anticipation. The site is spread over a vast area, and much of it remains unexcavated, hidden beneath the thick canopy of trees. This setting lends Coba an almost untouched quality, making the exploration feel like a genuine adventure.

The centerpiece of Coba is Nohoch Mul, the tallest pyramid in the Yucatán Peninsula. Standing at about 42 meters (138 feet), it's an imposing structure that towers above the jungle. Unlike many other pyramids in the region, visitors are allowed to climb to the top of Nohoch Mul. The ascent is steep and can be challenging, especially on a hot day, but the effort is well worth it. From the summit, you're rewarded with a breathtaking view of the surrounding jungle, a sea of green stretching as far as the eye can see. It's a perspective that gives you a true sense of the scale and grandeur of the ancient city.

Coba is unique among Mayan sites for its extensive network of sacbeob, or white roads. These ancient causeways, made of limestone, radiate out from the city center like spokes on a wheel. The longest sacbe connects Coba to the ancient city of Yaxuná, over 100 kilometers away. Walking along these ancient roads, you can almost imagine the hustle and bustle of a once-thriving metropolis, with traders, travelers, and priests moving between cities.

The site is also home to several impressive stelae, tall stone slabs carved with images and glyphs. These stelae document important events, such as battles and ceremonies, and provide valuable insights into the social and political life of the Maya. One particularly notable stele, Stele 1, depicts a ruler in elaborate attire, underscoring the city's importance as a political and ceremonial center.

Coba's layout reflects the Maya's deep connection to their environment and their sophisticated urban planning. The city is built around a series of lagoons, which provided a vital water source. These lagoons, now home to a variety of wildlife, add to the site's natural beauty. The tranquility of the water, combined with the dense foliage and the distant calls of birds and monkeys, creates a serene atmosphere that contrasts with the monumental architecture.

As you wander through Coba, the sense of exploration is palpable. Bicycles and tricycles are available for rent, allowing you to cover more ground and discover the site's hidden corners. Pedaling along the shaded paths, you can stumble upon smaller structures, such as the ball courts where the Maya played their ritualistic games, and residential areas that hint at the daily lives of the inhabitants.

One of the most striking aspects of Coba is how it merges with the jungle. Trees grow through the ancient stones, and vines drape over ruins, creating a sense of nature reclaiming history. This integration of the natural and the man-made gives Coba a unique character and a raw, untouched beauty that is rare in more frequently visited sites.

Visiting Coba is a journey not just through space, but through time. It's a place where you can feel the pulse of ancient life and the enduring presence of the natural world. The site's remoteness and its less-visited status make it a more intimate and personal experience, one where you can truly immerse yourself in the mystery and majesty of the Maya civilization.

Whether you're climbing the heights of Nohoch Mul, tracing the routes of the sacbeob, or simply soaking in the serene beauty of the lagoons, Coba offers an exploration that is both enriching and unforgettable. It's a reminder of the ingenuity, resilience, and spirit of the Maya, and a place where history lives on in every stone and tree.

Ek Balam

Ek Balam, which translates to "Black Jaguar" in Maya, is a mesmerizing archaeological site nestled in the heart of the Yucatán Peninsula. Unlike its more famous counterparts, Chichén Itzá and Tulum, Ek Balam offers a more intimate and less crowded exploration, allowing visitors to truly immerse themselves in the ancient world of the Maya.

The journey to Ek Balam starts with a sense of excitement, as the site is surrounded by lush jungle and hidden away from the hustle and bustle of more popular tourist destinations. Upon arrival, the first thing that captures your attention is the well-preserved state of the ruins. The site has only been partially excavated, which adds to its mysterious charm.

The centerpiece of Ek Balam is the Acropolis, one of the largest structures in the Yucatán. This towering pyramid stretches over 500 feet in length, and climbing its steep steps is a rewarding challenge. As you ascend, intricate stucco sculptures and carvings come into view, depicting scenes from Mayan mythology and history. The most striking feature is the entrance to the tomb of Ukit Kan Le'k Tok', a powerful ruler whose tomb is adorned with detailed and expressive figures. This facade, known as the "monster mouth," represents the entrance to the underworld and is guarded by fierce carvings of jaguars and serpents.

From the top of the Acropolis, the panoramic views are breathtaking. The vast expanse of jungle stretches out before you, with other pyramids and structures peeking through the canopy. This vantage point offers a sense of the scale and significance of Ek Balam as a major city in the Maya civilization.

Wandering through the site, you'll encounter various structures that reveal the complexity and sophistication of Ek Balam. The Oval Palace, with its distinctive rounded shape, served as a residence for high-ranking officials and offers a glimpse into the daily lives of the Maya elite. The Ball Court, where the Maya played their ritualistic ball game, stands as a testament to the cultural and religious importance of this ancient sport.

One of the unique aspects of Ek Balam is its relatively recent discovery and excavation. The site was largely unknown to the outside world until the late 20th century, and much of it remains untouched by modern hands. This sense of being a pioneer in uncovering ancient history adds an element of adventure to your visit.

The surrounding jungle plays a significant role in the experience of Ek Balam. The site is alive with the sounds of nature, from the chirping of birds to the rustling of leaves in the breeze. This natural soundtrack, combined with the sight of trees growing through and around the ruins, creates a serene and almost mystical atmosphere.

As you explore Ek Balam, it's easy to imagine the city as it once was—a bustling hub of activity, with priests performing rituals, traders exchanging goods, and citizens going about their daily lives. The site offers a deeply personal connection to the past, as if you're walking in the footsteps of the ancient Maya.

For those looking to extend their adventure, the nearby cenote, X'Canche, provides a refreshing escape. This natural sinkhole, filled with crystal-clear water, is perfect for a swim after a day of exploring the ruins. The cenote is reached by a short bike ride or walk through the jungle, adding another layer of exploration to your visit.

Ek Balam is a place where history and nature converge, offering a unique and enriching experience for those willing to venture off the beaten path. It's a site that invites you to uncover the secrets of the past and to appreciate the timeless beauty of the natural world. Whether you're an avid historian, a nature lover, or simply a curious traveler, Ek Balam promises a journey of discovery and wonder.

Other Notable Ruins

Exploring the Yucatán Peninsula reveals a treasure trove of ancient ruins, each with its own unique charm and historical significance. Beyond the well-known sites of Chichén Itzá, Uxmal, Coba, and Ek Balam, there are several other remarkable ruins that offer a deeper dive into the rich tapestry of Mayan civilization.

Kabah, located along the Puuc Route, is an impressive site known for its elaborate stone carvings and architecture. The highlight here is the Palace of the Masks, adorned with hundreds of stone masks dedicated to the rain god Chaac. Walking through Kabah, you can sense the importance of water to the Maya, reflected in the intricate designs and the sheer number of masks.

Not far from Kabah is Sayil, another gem along the Puuc Route. Sayil is smaller than some of the other sites, but it's no less fascinating. The grand palace, with its three stories and numerous rooms, showcases the architectural prowess of the Maya. Exploring Sayil, you get a sense of a bustling community that once thrived here, with homes, temples, and public spaces that paint a picture of daily life.

Labná, also part of the Puuc Route, stands out for its stunning archway, one of the most photographed structures in the region. The arch is not just a beautiful piece of architecture but also a symbol of the Maya's engineering skills. Nearby, the El Mirador temple offers panoramic views of the surrounding landscape, providing a glimpse into the strategic placement of Maya cities.

Heading north, the site of Dzibilchaltún offers a fascinating mix of history and natural beauty. The Temple of the Seven Dolls is the centerpiece here, named for the seven small effigies found during excavation. This temple is aligned with the sun, and during the equinoxes, the sunrise shines directly through its doors, creating a magical effect. After exploring the ruins, a dip in the cenote Xlacah, located within the site, offers a refreshing break.

Further south, Xpujil is part of the lesser-known Río Bec region, characterized by its distinctive architectural style. The site features several impressive structures, including the Palace of Xpujil, with its three towers and intricate stone carvings. Xpujil is less frequented by tourists, allowing for a more tranquil and immersive experience.

Kohunlich, located near the border with Belize, is another notable site. It's famous for its Temple of the Masks, which features large stucco masks of the sun god Kinich Ahau. These masks are remarkably well-preserved and offer a vivid glimpse into the religious practices of the Maya. The surrounding jungle adds to the allure, creating a sense of discovery as you explore the site.

Edzná, near Campeche, is known for its impressive five-story palace and extensive hydraulic system. The Great Acropolis dominates the site, with its commanding views and intricate carvings. Edzná's sophisticated system of canals and reservoirs reflects the Maya's advanced understanding of water management, essential for supporting a large urban population.

Exploring these lesser-known ruins provides a more intimate connection with the past and allows you to appreciate the diversity and ingenuity of the Maya civilization. Each site tells a different story, from grand political centers to smaller, but no less important, communities. The Yucatán Peninsula is a living museum, and its ruins are open chapters waiting to be discovered. Whether you're an avid historian, an architecture enthusiast, or a curious traveler, these sites offer a journey through time that is both enriching and unforgettable.

Cenotes and Natural Wonders

What are Cenotes?

Cenotes are one of the Yucatán Peninsula's most enchanting natural features. These natural sinkholes, filled with crystal-clear groundwater, have captivated locals and travelers alike for centuries. The word "cenote" comes from the Mayan term "dzonot," meaning "well," and these formations played a crucial role in the region's ancient and modern life.

Formed by the collapse of limestone bedrock, cenotes reveal the water table below. The Yucatán is riddled with them, thanks to its porous karst landscape. Some are open to the sky, while others are hidden within caves, creating a diverse array of environments to explore.

For the ancient Maya, cenotes were sacred. They were believed to be portals to the underworld and were often used for rituals and offerings. Many cenotes have yielded fascinating archaeological finds, including pottery, jewelry, and even human remains, all offering insights into the spiritual lives of the Maya.

Today, cenotes are natural playgrounds. The water is often refreshingly cool, a welcome respite from the tropical heat. Swimming in a cenote is like entering a different world. The water is so clear that you can see the intricate rock formations and fish swimming below. Sunlight filters through the openings, casting an otherworldly glow.

Different types of cenotes offer unique experiences. Open cenotes, like Cenote Azul, are entirely exposed to the sky and often surrounded by lush vegetation, making them perfect for a swim or a picnic. Semi-open cenotes, such as Cenote Ik Kil near Chichén Itzá, have partially collapsed roofs, creating dramatic settings with hanging vines and deep blue waters.

Then there are the cave cenotes, like Dos Ojos near Tulum, which offer more adventurous experiences. Equipped with snorkeling or diving gear, you can explore the underwater caverns and tunnels, marveling at the stalactites and stalagmites formed over millennia. These cenotes require a bit more effort to access but reward you with a sense of awe and discovery.

Visiting a cenote is an intimate way to connect with the Yucatán's natural beauty. Whether you're swimming, snorkeling, or just floating on your back, gazing up at the canopy or cave ceiling, it's an experience that brings you closer to the wonders of the natural world. And knowing that these waters have been revered for centuries adds a layer of depth to the experience, making it not just a swim, but a journey through time and nature.

So, when you find yourself in the Yucatán, take the plunge into a cenote. It's a refreshing dip into history, nature, and the mystique of the ancient Maya. Enjoy the serene beauty, the clear waters, and the sense of adventure that comes with exploring these incredible natural formations. The experience is sure to leave you with memories that linger long after you've dried off.

Top Cenotes to Visit

The Yucatán Peninsula is home to thousands of cenotes, each offering a unique experience. Here are some of the top cenotes you might want to check out:

Cenote Ik Kil, located near Chichén Itzá, is famous for its stunning beauty and is a popular spot for swimming and snorkeling. The clear blue water and the lush vegetation around it make it a photographer's paradise.

Cenote Azul is known for its deep blue waters, perfect for a refreshing swim. It's located near Tulum and is surrounded by jungle, giving it a secluded and tranquil feel.

Cenote Dos Ojos is part of a large underwater cave system and offers the chance for guided cave diving tours. It's a bit more adventurous and is great for those who love exploring underwater.

Cenote Calavera, located near Tulum, is known for its unique skull-like appearance due to the rock formations around it. It's a popular spot for swimming and diving.

Cenote Suytun is famous for its iconic stone path leading to the water and the sunlight streaming through the opening above, creating a magical atmosphere.

Cenote Zací, situated in the town of Valladolid, is a great spot for a swim and is surrounded by historical ruins, adding an extra layer of intrigue.

Cenote Hubiku, located near Coba, is less crowded and offers a peaceful environment for swimming and relaxing.

Cenote Cristalino, near Playa del Carmen, is known for its crystal-clear waters and is a great spot for snorkeling and enjoying the underwater scenery.

Cenote Chaak Tun, located near Tulum, offers guided tours that take you through the cave system, providing a unique and adventurous experience.

Cenote Palomitas is part of a small group of cenotes near Coba and is known for its beautiful, clear waters and the surrounding jungle.

Each of these cenotes offers a different experience, from the adventurous dives in Dos Ojos to the serene beauty of Cenote Azul. Exploring these natural wonders is a fantastic way to connect with the natural beauty and history of the Yucatán Peninsula. Have you visited any cenotes before, or is this your first time exploring them?

Caves and Underground Rivers

The Yucatán Peninsula is a geological wonder, home to an extensive network of caves and underground rivers that have shaped the region's landscape and history. These subterranean worlds offer a unique adventure for those willing to delve beneath the surface and explore their hidden wonders.

One of the most famous cave systems in the Yucatán is Rio Secreto. Located near Playa del Carmen, this "Secret River" lives up to its name with its labyrinth of underground passageways and crystal-clear waters. Guided tours lead you through the caves, where you wade and swim in knee-deep water, marveling at the stunning stalactites and stalagmites that adorn the cavern walls. The ethereal beauty of the underground formations, combined with the sense of mystery and adventure, makes Rio Secreto a must-visit.

Actun Chen, another remarkable cave system, offers a blend of natural beauty and ancient history. This site, located near

Tulum, features a series of caves that have been used by the Maya for centuries. The guided tours take you through well-lit caverns filled with spectacular rock formations and underground pools. The highlight is the Cenote Chen, a breathtaking subterranean lake that adds to the mystique of the caves.

The Sac Actun system, part of the world's longest underwater cave system, is a paradise for divers and snorkelers. This expansive network of submerged caverns stretches for over 350 kilometers and offers a glimpse into an alien-like underwater world. Divers can explore the vast tunnels and chambers, where the water is so clear that it feels like floating in air. The flora and fauna in these waters are unique, making it an unparalleled experience for those seeking underwater adventures.

Gran Cenote, located near Tulum, is another highlight. This cenote is part of a larger cave system and offers both snorkeling and diving opportunities. The cenote is surrounded by lush greenery and features crystal-clear water that reveals intricate cave formations just below the surface. Swimming through the caves, you can encounter turtles and a variety of fish, adding a touch of wildlife to the subterranean experience.

Dzitnup, also known as Cenote X'keken, near Valladolid, is famed for its dramatic cave setting. The cavern, illuminated by a single shaft of sunlight that pierces through an opening in the roof, creates a magical and serene environment. The stalactites hanging from the ceiling and the crystal-clear blue water below make for an enchanting swim.

The caves and underground rivers of the Yucatán Peninsula are not just natural wonders; they are also windows into the region's past. These formations have been used for centuries by the Maya for rituals and as sources of fresh water. Artifacts, bones, and pottery found within the caves provide a glimpse into ancient life and beliefs.

Exploring these subterranean landscapes requires a sense of adventure and a respect for the natural environment. Guided tours are essential, as they ensure safety and provide fascinating insights into the geology and history of the caves. Whether you're walking through illuminated caverns or diving into the depths of an underwater cave, the experience is both thrilling and humbling.

The Yucatán's caves and underground rivers offer a journey into a hidden world, where every rock formation and shadow tells a story. It's a chance to see the region from a different perspective, one that reveals the incredible power of nature and the enduring legacy of the ancient Maya. So, don your wetsuit, grab a flashlight, and get ready to explore the subterranean splendor of the Yucatán Peninsula.

Nature Reserves and Parks

The Yucatán Peninsula isn't just about ancient ruins and vibrant cities; it's also a treasure trove of natural beauty, teeming with diverse ecosystems. Exploring the region's nature reserves and parks gives you a chance to witness its rich biodiversity and serene landscapes firsthand.

One of the most celebrated reserves is Sian Ka'an Biosphere Reserve, a UNESCO World Heritage site. Located near Tulum, Sian Ka'an spans over 1.3 million acres, encompassing tropical forests, mangroves, and marine areas. It's a haven for wildlife enthusiasts, offering the chance to see jaguars, manatees, and a plethora of bird species. Taking a boat tour through the reserve's waterways is an unforgettable experience, where you can spot dolphins frolicking and explore ancient Mayan canals.

Calakmul Biosphere Reserve, another UNESCO site, is located deeper in the jungle, near the Guatemalan border. This vast reserve is home to the ruins of Calakmul, one of the largest Mayan cities. Beyond the historical significance, the reserve is a biodiversity hotspot. Towering trees, exotic plants, and an array of animals, including monkeys and toucans, make this a paradise for nature lovers. Hiking through the lush jungle trails, you'll feel like you've stepped back in time.

Celestún Biosphere Reserve, situated on the Gulf of Mexico, is famed for its flamingo colonies. The shallow coastal lagoons and estuaries provide an ideal habitat for these striking pink birds. A boat tour through the reserve lets you get up close to the flamingos, as well as other wildlife like pelicans, herons, and crocodiles. The reserve's mangroves and freshwater springs add to the diversity of the landscape.

Ría Lagartos Biosphere Reserve, located on the northern coast of the peninsula, is another prime destination for birdwatching. Besides flamingos, the reserve is home to over 300 bird species, including spoonbills and kingfishers. The salt flats and mangroves create a unique environment that's both beautiful and ecologically important. Boat tours are a great way to explore the waterways and observe the abundant wildlife.

For a different kind of natural beauty, the Reserva de la Biósfera de Los Petenes, near the city of Campeche, offers an intriguing mix of ecosystems. This reserve features extensive wetlands, tropical forests, and coastal areas. The Petenes are unique wetlands formed by freshwater springs within the mangroves, creating a distinct habitat for many plant and animal species. Exploring this reserve, either by boat or on foot, gives you a glimpse into the complexity and interconnectedness of the region's ecosystems.

Punta Laguna Nature Reserve, located near Coba, is a smaller but equally captivating spot. It's renowned for its spider monkey population and offers guided tours that take you through the jungle to see these playful creatures in their natural habitat. The reserve also features a beautiful lagoon, perfect for kayaking, and cenotes for swimming. The combination of wildlife encounters and serene landscapes makes Punta Laguna a hidden gem.

Lastly, the Xcaret Park, near Playa del Carmen, combines natural beauty with cultural experiences. While it's more commercial than the other reserves, Xcaret offers a blend of ecological and archaeological attractions. You can snorkel in underground rivers, explore butterfly pavilions, and learn about Mayan history and traditions through performances and exhibits. It's a family-friendly destination that provides a taste of the region's diverse offerings.

Exploring the nature reserves and parks of the Yucatán Peninsula is a journey into the heart of its ecological and cultural richness. Each reserve offers a unique window into the natural world, from vibrant bird colonies to dense jungles teeming with wildlife. Whether you're gliding through mangroves, hiking ancient trails, or simply soaking in the serene beauty, these protected areas provide unforgettable experiences and a deeper appreciation of the Yucatán's natural wonders.

Eco-Tourism Activities

The Yucatán Peninsula is a haven for eco-tourism, offering numerous opportunities to immerse yourself in nature while supporting sustainable travel practices. Here are some top eco-tourism activities that highlight the region's natural beauty and biodiversity:

1. **Birdwatching in Celestún Biosphere Reserve:** Celestún is renowned for its flamingo colonies and diverse bird species. Taking a guided boat tour through the mangroves and estuaries allows you to spot flamingos, pelicans, herons, and countless other birds. The reserve's focus on conservation and habitat protection makes it an excellent destination for eco-conscious travelers.

2. **Exploring Sian Ka'an Biosphere Reserve:** Sian Ka'an, a UNESCO World Heritage site, offers a range of eco-tourism activities. You can take a boat tour through the mangroves, kayak along ancient Mayan canals, or snorkel in the crystal-clear waters of the Caribbean. The reserve's commitment to preserving its diverse ecosystems ensures that your visit supports local conservation efforts.

3. **Swimming and Snorkeling in Cenotes:** The cenotes of the Yucatán are natural wonders that provide a unique and refreshing experience. Swimming in these crystal-clear sinkholes connects you with the region's geological history and

helps sustain eco-tourism efforts aimed at preserving these fragile environments. Cenotes like Dos Ojos, Gran Cenote, and Cenote Azul are popular choices.

4. Hiking and Wildlife Watching in Calakmul Biosphere Reserve: Calakmul offers a combination of historical exploration and nature immersion. Hiking through the dense jungle, you can encounter a variety of wildlife, including howler monkeys, jaguars, and toucans. The reserve's focus on protecting endangered species and their habitats makes it a vital eco-tourism destination.

5. Kayaking in the Lagoons of Ría Lagartos: Ría Lagartos Biosphere Reserve is another prime spot for eco-tourism. Kayaking through the tranquil lagoons and mangroves allows you to get up close to the region's wildlife, including flamingos, crocodiles, and countless bird species. The reserve's emphasis on sustainable tourism ensures that your visit benefits the local environment.

6. Cycling Tours in Valladolid: Valladolid is a charming colonial town that serves as a gateway to various eco-tourism activities. Renting a bike and exploring the town and its surroundings promotes sustainable travel. You can cycle to nearby cenotes, such as Cenote Zací, or visit the eco-friendly archaeological site of Ek Balam.

7. Participating in Conservation Projects: Many eco-tourism operators in the Yucatán offer opportunities to participate in conservation projects. Whether it's volunteering at a sea turtle sanctuary, assisting with reforestation efforts, or supporting wildlife monitoring programs, these activities allow you to make a positive impact on the environment while gaining a deeper understanding of local conservation efforts.

8. Visiting Eco-Friendly Resorts and Lodges: The Yucatán boasts several eco-friendly accommodations that prioritize sustainability. Staying at an eco-lodge or resort not only reduces your environmental footprint but also supports local communities and conservation initiatives. Many of these establishments offer guided nature walks, birdwatching tours, and cultural experiences that enhance your eco-tourism adventure.

Engaging in eco-tourism activities in the Yucatán Peninsula allows you to experience the region's natural wonders while contributing to the preservation of its unique ecosystems. Whether you're kayaking through mangroves, exploring ancient ruins, or swimming in cenotes, your eco-conscious choices help ensure that future generations can enjoy the beauty and biodiversity of this remarkable area.

Yucatan Cuisine

Traditional Dishes

The culinary journey through the Yucatán Peninsula is one filled with rich flavors and deep-rooted traditions. Yucatecan cuisine is a blend of Mayan, Spanish, Caribbean, and even Middle Eastern influences, resulting in a unique and delicious food culture. Here are some traditional dishes you simply must try:

Cochinita Pibil is a dish that perfectly captures the essence of Yucatán's culinary heritage. Traditionally, a whole pig is marinated in achiote (a spice made from annatto seeds), sour orange juice, and a blend of spices. It's then wrapped in banana leaves and slow-cooked in a pit oven known as a "pib." The result is tender, flavorful meat that falls apart at the touch. Served with pickled red onions and habanero salsa, cochinita pibil is often enjoyed with corn tortillas, making for a hearty and satisfying meal.

Another must-try dish is Sopa de Lima, or lime soup. This aromatic and refreshing soup features shredded chicken, a light broth flavored with lime juice, and crisp tortilla strips. The addition of fragrant herbs and spices gives it a distinct and zesty taste that is both comforting and invigorating. It's a perfect starter or a light meal, especially on a warm day.

Papadzules are a delicious and traditional Yucatecan dish. Often considered the precursor to enchiladas, papadzules are corn tortillas filled with hard-boiled eggs and topped with a rich pumpkin seed sauce. They're usually garnished with a tomato sauce that adds a subtle sweetness, balancing out the nuttiness of the pumpkin seeds. This dish is simple yet incredibly flavorful, and it's a staple in many local households.

Tamales are ubiquitous throughout Mexico, but the Yucatán has its own special versions. One such variety is the Tamal Colado, which is made with a smooth, strained masa (corn dough) filled with seasoned chicken or pork. These tamales are wrapped in banana leaves and steamed, resulting in a dish that is both moist and packed with flavor. The banana leaves impart a unique taste that distinguishes Yucatecan tamales from other regional varieties.

Huevos Motuleños is a popular breakfast dish that hails from the town of Motul. It consists of a fried tortilla topped with black beans, a fried egg, and a tomato-based sauce. The dish is often garnished with peas, ham, and plantains, making for a hearty and colorful breakfast. The combination of flavors and textures makes it a delightful way to start the day.

Another notable dish is Relleno Negro, a rich and flavorful stew made with turkey and a blackened spice mixture called recado negro. The dark color comes from charred chiles and other ingredients ground into a paste. The stew is hearty and complex, with a smoky depth of flavor that is enhanced by the slow-cooking process. It's typically served with rice or corn tortillas, making it a satisfying and comforting meal.

Panuchos and Salbutes are beloved street foods in the Yucatán. Both are made with fried tortillas, but they have distinct differences. Panuchos are stuffed with refried black beans before being fried and topped with shredded turkey or chicken, pickled onions, avocado, and lettuce. Salbutes, on the other hand, are not stuffed but simply topped with similar ingredients. Both are crispy, savory, and perfect for a quick snack or light meal.

No culinary journey through the Yucatán would be complete without sampling some of the region's sweets. One such treat is Marquesitas, a type of crunchy crepe filled with local cheese and sweet fillings like chocolate or caramel. These are often sold by street vendors and make for a delightful dessert or snack. The combination of the savory cheese and the sweet filling creates a unique and irresistible flavor.

To wash it all down, try Agua de Chaya, a refreshing drink made from the leaves of the chaya plant, also known as tree spinach. Blended with lime juice and sometimes pineapple, this drink is not only delicious but also packed with nutrients. It's a perfect way to cool off and rehydrate after exploring the hot and humid landscape of the Yucatán.

Each of these dishes tells a story of the region's rich culinary history and cultural influences. Whether you're dining at a high-end restaurant or enjoying street food, the flavors of the Yucatán will leave a lasting impression. So dig in, savor each bite, and enjoy the delicious adventure that is Yucatecan cuisine.

Must-Try Street Food

Exploring street food in the Yucatán Peninsula is an adventure for your taste buds. The flavors are bold, the ingredients fresh, and the culinary traditions deeply rooted in the region's culture. Here are some must-try street foods that capture the essence of Yucatecan cuisine:

Start with Salbutes. These are puffed, fried tortillas topped with shredded turkey or chicken, lettuce, avocado, pickled red onions, and sometimes a slice of hard-boiled egg. The combination of crispy tortilla and fresh toppings makes for a satisfying snack.

Panuchos are similar but have a twist. These tortillas are stuffed with refried black beans before being fried, then topped with turkey or chicken, pickled onions, and avocado. The added layer of beans gives panuchos a richer, heartier flavor.

For breakfast or a light meal, try Cochinita Pibil Tacos. Cochinita pibil is slow-roasted pork marinated in achiote and citrus, wrapped in banana leaves, and cooked until tender. The pork is then shredded and served in corn tortillas, topped with pickled red onions and a squeeze of lime. The meat is incredibly flavorful, and the tangy onions add a perfect contrast.

Another popular snack is Empanadas de Chaya. These are made with masa (corn dough) mixed with chaya, a local green leafy vegetable similar to spinach. The masa is filled with cheese or other fillings and fried until golden brown. They're crispy on the outside, soft on the inside, and very nutritious.

Don't miss out on Sopa de Lima, a lime soup that's refreshing and aromatic. It's made with shredded chicken, a light chicken broth, and lime juice, topped with fried tortilla strips. It's often served as an appetizer but can be enjoyed as a light meal on its own.

Elotes are a favorite street food throughout Mexico, and the Yucatán is no exception. These are grilled corn on the cob, typically slathered with mayonnaise, cotija cheese, chili powder, and lime juice. The combination of smoky, sweet, and tangy flavors makes elotes a hit.

When it comes to desserts, Marquesitas are a must-try. These crispy crepes are rolled up with fillings such as Nutella, caramel, or local cheese. They're a popular treat, often sold from street carts. The mix of sweet and savory in the cheese-filled ones is particularly delightful.

For a refreshing beverage, look for Agua de Chaya. This is a drink made from the chaya plant, blended with lime juice and sometimes pineapple. It's not only delicious but also very healthy, packed with vitamins and minerals.

Street food in the Yucatán Peninsula offers a vibrant and flavorful experience that's as diverse as the region itself. Whether you're munching on panuchos at a local market or sipping on agua de chaya from a street vendor, these culinary delights are sure to leave you with a taste of Yucatán's rich culinary heritage. Enjoy every bite and sip, and savor the unique flavors of this incredible region.

Regional Specialties

The Yucatán Peninsula boasts a culinary landscape that's as rich and diverse as its history and culture. From hearty stews to refreshing beverages, the region's specialties offer a delightful exploration of flavors and traditions.

One of the standout dishes is Cochinita Pibil, a signature Yucatecan dish that's deeply rooted in Mayan traditions. This dish involves marinating pork in achiote paste, sour orange juice, and a blend of spices, then wrapping it in banana leaves and slow-cooking it in a pit oven. The result is succulent, flavorful meat that's typically served with pickled red onions and fresh corn tortillas. It's a must-try for anyone visiting the region.

Poc Chuc is another beloved specialty. This dish consists of grilled pork marinated in a sour orange juice and garlic mixture. The tangy flavor of the marinade balances perfectly with the smokiness from the grill. Poc Chuc is usually served with rice, black beans, pickled onions, and a side of fresh tortillas.

Queso Relleno highlights the region's blend of cultures. This dish features a hollowed-out Edam cheese filled with a mixture of minced pork, almonds, raisins, and spices, then baked until the cheese melts. It's topped with a rich tomato sauce and served with a side of rice. The combination of savory, sweet, and spicy flavors makes it a unique and delightful experience.

For seafood lovers, Tikin Xic is a must. This traditional dish involves marinating fish in achiote paste and sour orange juice, then wrapping it in banana leaves and grilling it to perfection. The fish is tender and flavorful, with a hint of smokiness from the grill. It's typically served with rice, beans, and fresh tortillas.

Relleno Negro is a rich, hearty stew that showcases the complexity of Yucatecan flavors. Made with turkey and a blackened spice mixture called recado negro, the stew has a deep, smoky flavor. The black color comes from charred chiles and other ingredients ground into a paste. This dish is often enjoyed during special occasions and holidays, and it's usually served with rice or tortillas.

Another noteworthy dish is Pan de Cazón, which features layers of corn tortillas and shredded shark meat, topped with a tomato sauce and garnished with fresh herbs. This dish reflects the coastal influences on Yucatecan cuisine and offers a unique taste of the sea.

For a taste of traditional Yucatecan breakfast, try Huevos Motuleños. This dish consists of fried tortillas topped with black beans, a fried egg, and a tomato-based sauce. It's garnished with peas, ham, and plantains, making for a hearty and colorful start to the day.

When it comes to beverages, Horchata de Arroz con Coco is a refreshing choice. This drink is made from rice milk blended with coconut milk, cinnamon, and sugar. It's served chilled and provides a sweet, creamy respite from the tropical heat.

Lastly, don't miss out on Sopa de Lima, a fragrant lime soup made with shredded chicken, a light broth, and crisp tortilla strips. The addition of fragrant herbs and fresh lime juice gives it a distinct and zesty flavor, making it a perfect appetizer or light meal.

These regional specialties offer a delicious journey through the Yucatán Peninsula's culinary heritage. Each dish tells a story of the region's history, blending indigenous ingredients with influences from across the globe. Enjoying these flavors is more than just eating; it's a way to connect with the rich culture and traditions of the Yucatán.

Food Festivals and Events

The Yucatán Peninsula is a vibrant hub of cultural celebrations and food festivals that showcase the region's rich culinary heritage and traditions. Here are some notable events that food enthusiasts should look out for:

Mérida Fest is held every January to celebrate the founding of Mérida. This month-long festival features a variety of events, including dance performances, visual arts showings, and gallery openings. The festivities kick off with the Alborada, a march through the city, and culminate with the Mañanitas, a traditional birthday song performed at midnight on January 6.

Carnaval de Mérida takes place in February and is similar to Mardi Gras. It features parades, music, dance, and lots of food. The streets come alive with colorful floats, costumes, and street vendors offering a variety of traditional Yucatecan dishes.

The National Edam Cheese (Queso de Bola) Festival celebrates the beloved Edam cheese, a staple in Yucatecan cuisine. Held in different locations, including the main square in Motul, the festival highlights street food, traditional dishes, and creative inventions made from Edam cheese.

The Ice Cream Festival in Yucatán is perfect for cooling off during the hot summer months. This festival offers a variety of ice creams, popsicles, frappés, and desserts. You'll also find handcrafts, live music, and typical Yucatecan food, making it a fun and refreshing event.

The Halachó Fair is celebrated in July and August and honors the Apostle Santiago (St. James) with pilgrimages, Masses, dances, music, and a local fair. It's a great opportunity to experience the local culture and enjoy traditional Yucatecan cuisine.

The San Felipe Village Fair takes place in the town of San Felipe and features a variety of traditional foods, crafts, and cultural performances. It's a great way to immerse yourself in the local culture and taste some authentic Yucatecan dishes.

Spring and Autumn Equinox Festivals at Chichén Itzá are held at the Temple of Kukulkán. During these festivals, the pyramid aligns with the sun, creating a unique shadow effect. The event attracts thousands of visitors who come to witness this phenomenon and enjoy traditional food and music.

These festivals and events offer a fantastic way to experience the culinary delights and cultural richness of the Yucatán Peninsula. Whether you're sampling traditional dishes, enjoying live music, or participating in local customs, you're sure to have an unforgettable time.

Cooking Classes and Culinary Tours

Cooking classes and culinary tours in the Yucatán Peninsula offer a flavorful way to connect with the region's rich culinary heritage. These hands-on experiences allow you to dive into the heart of Yucatecan cuisine, learning from local chefs and exploring traditional markets.

In Mérida, the capital of Yucatán, several cooking schools offer immersive classes that take you through the preparation of iconic dishes like cochinita pibil, sopa de lima, and tamales. You'll start with a visit to the bustling markets, where you'll pick out fresh ingredients and learn about the unique spices and herbs that define Yucatecan flavors. Back in the kitchen, local chefs guide you through each step, sharing techniques passed down through generations. The best part, of course, is sitting down to enjoy the meal you've created, often accompanied by traditional drinks like agua de chaya or horchata.

Culinary tours in the region go beyond the kitchen. In Valladolid, a charming colonial town, you can join food tours that weave through cobblestone streets and vibrant plazas. These tours often include stops at local eateries and street vendors, where you can taste specialties like panuchos, salbutes, and marquesitas. Along the way, knowledgeable guides share stories about the town's history and culinary traditions, adding depth to each bite.

In the coastal areas, culinary tours often highlight the abundance of fresh seafood. Tulum and Playa del Carmen offer seafood-focused experiences, where you can learn to prepare dishes like tikin xic, a marinated fish grilled in banana leaves, and ceviche made with the catch of the day. These tours often include a visit to local fishing villages, where you can see the day's catch being brought in and meet the fishermen who supply the region's markets.

For a more hands-on experience, some eco-lodges and resorts in the region offer cooking classes as part of their activities.

These classes often focus on farm-to-table practices, using ingredients grown on-site or sourced from nearby farms. You'll learn to cook with seasonal produce, exploring the connections between food, culture, and the land.

The Yucatán Peninsula's rich culinary scene is also celebrated through various food festivals and events. Attending these can be a delightful way to immerse yourself in local flavors and culinary traditions. Events like the Mérida Fest and the National Edam Cheese Festival offer a chance to sample a wide variety of dishes, participate in cooking demonstrations, and meet local chefs and food producers.

Whether you're a seasoned cook looking to expand your culinary repertoire or simply a food lover eager to taste the flavors of the Yucatán, cooking classes and culinary tours provide an enriching and delicious way to experience the region. Each class and tour is a journey into the heart of Yucatecan cuisine, where every ingredient has a story and every dish is a celebration of the region's vibrant culinary heritage.

Top Ten Cities to Visit

Merida

Merida, the vibrant capital of Yucatan, is a treasure trove of history, culture, and natural beauty. Let's dive into some of the must-visit attractions and what you need to know about each one.

Plaza Grande is the heart of the city. Surrounded by iconic buildings like the San Ildefonso Cathedral and the Governor's Palace, it's a perfect spot to people-watch and soak in the colonial charm. The square is open 24/7, and there's no entry fee.

Casa de Montejo, built in 1549, offers a glimpse into the life of the city's founder. The museum is open Tuesday to Saturday from 10:00 AM to 5:00 PM, and Sunday from 10:00 AM to 2:00 PM. Entry is free, but donations are appreciated.

San Ildefonso Cathedral is one of the oldest cathedrals in the Americas and a stunning example of colonial architecture. The cathedral is open daily from 9:00 AM to 6:00 PM, and there's no entry fee.

Paseo de Montejo, a grand boulevard lined with beautiful mansions, offers a lovely stroll. It's open to the public at all times, and you can enjoy the scenery without any cost.

Parque de Santa Lucia is a charming park with lush greenery and a picturesque lake. It's a great place to relax and enjoy a picnic. The park is open daily from 5:00 AM to 10:00 PM, and there's no entry fee.

The Macay Museum showcases a vast collection of pre-Hispanic artifacts. It's open Tuesday to Saturday from 9:30 AM to 6:30 PM, and Sunday from 10:00 AM to 3:00 PM. The entry fee is around 50 pesos.

Palacio Canton, a beautiful building that now houses the Museum of the City of Merida, is open Tuesday to Sunday from 9:00 AM to 6:00 PM. The entry fee is around 50 pesos.

The Museum of the Mayan World offers an in-depth look at the ancient Maya civilization. It's open Tuesday to Sunday from 9:00 AM to 6:00 PM, and the entry fee is around 70 pesos.

Celestun, a small town known for its flamingo population and beautiful beaches, is a great day trip from Merida. You can enjoy the natural beauty without any entry fee.

Uxmal, one of the most impressive Mayan archaeological sites, is a must-visit. It's open daily from 8:00 AM to 5:00 PM, and the entry fee is around 70 pesos.

Merida is a city that offers something for everyone, from history enthusiasts to nature lovers. Enjoy your visit and make the most of everything this beautiful city has to offer!

Cancun

Cancun, a gem on the Yucatan Peninsula, is a paradise for travelers seeking sun, sea, and culture. Let's dive into some of the top attractions and what you need to know about each one.

Hotel Zone (Zona Hotelera): This is where most visitors stay, with its long stretch of sandy beaches and all-inclusive resorts. You'll find plenty of restaurants, bars, and shops along Kukulcán Boulevard. It's a lively area perfect for beach lounging and nightlife.

Downtown Cancun (Ciudad Cancun): For a taste of local life, head to downtown Cancun. Wander down Avenida Tulum to experience the real Cancun with street food vendors, small shops, and green parks. It's a great spot to try authentic tacos and see a different side of the city.

Mayan Ruins of El Rey: Located in the Hotel Zone, these ancient ruins offer a glimpse into the region's rich history. The site is open daily from 8:00 AM to 5:00 PM, and the entry fee is around 70 pesos. It's a peaceful spot to explore and learn about the Maya civilization.

Cenote Dos Ojos: About 120 kilometers south of downtown Cancun, this stunning cenote is perfect for swimming, snorkeling, or cave diving. The park is open daily from 8:00 AM to 5:00 PM, and the entry fee is around 200 pesos. It's a magical experience to swim in the crystal-clear waters surrounded by stalactites.

Cancun Scenic Tower: For panoramic views of the city and coastline, visit the Cancun Scenic Tower. It's open daily from 9:00 AM to 6:00 PM, and the entry fee is around 100 pesos. The tower offers an elevator ride to the top, where you can enjoy breathtaking vistas.

Museo Maya de Cancun: This museum showcases an impressive collection of Mayan artifacts and offers insights into the ancient culture. It's open daily from 9:00 AM to 6:00 PM, and the entry fee is around 70 pesos. It's a fascinating place to learn about the region's history.

Isla Mujeres: Just a short ferry ride from Cancun, Isla Mujeres is a charming island known for its beautiful beaches and laid-back atmosphere. You can take a day trip to explore the island, visit the turtle sanctuary, and enjoy a relaxing day by the sea.

Xcaret Park: This eco-archaeological park offers a variety of activities, including underground rivers, caves, and a botanical garden. It's open daily from 8:00 AM to 6:00 PM, and the entry fee is around 700 pesos. It's a great place to experience the natural beauty and cultural heritage of the region.

Coco Bongo: For a night of entertainment, head to Coco Bongo, a popular nightclub in the Hotel Zone. It's open from 9:00 PM to 3:00 AM, and there's a cover charge of around 400 pesos. The club features live music, DJs, and acrobatic performances.

Playa Delfines: This beach is located in the Hotel Zone and is perfect for swimming and sunbathing. It's a beautiful spot to relax and enjoy the Caribbean Sea.

Cancun offers a mix of relaxation, adventure, and cultural experiences. Whether you're lounging on the beach, exploring ancient ruins, or enjoying the vibrant nightlife, there's something for everyone in this tropical paradise. Enjoy your time in Cancun!

Playa del Carmen

Playa del Carmen, a charming town on the Yucatan Peninsula, is a paradise for beach lovers and adventure seekers alike. Let's dive into some of the top attractions and what you need to know about each one.

La Quinta Avenida (5th Avenue): This lively pedestrian-only street is the heart of Playa del Carmen. Lined with shops, restaurants, bars, and street vendors, it's a great place to stroll, shop, and people-watch. You'll find everything from souvenirs and local handicrafts to designer boutiques and international brands. It's a bustling spot, especially in the evenings when street performers come out.

Playa del Carmen Beaches: The beaches here are some of the best in Mexico, with crystal-clear turquoise waters and soft white sand. Popular beaches include Playa Mamitas, Playa Norte, and Playa Caracol. These beaches are perfect for swimming, sunbathing, and enjoying water sports. Remember to bring sunscreen and stay hydrated!

Parque Los Fundadores: Located at the northern end of 5th Avenue, this park is a great spot to relax and enjoy the view of the Cozumel ferry pier. It's a popular gathering place for locals and tourists alike, with plenty of green space and benches.

Rio Secreto: This underground river and cave system offers a unique adventure. You can explore the stunning limestone formations, swim in the crystal-clear waters, and marvel at the natural beauty. Tours are available daily from 8:00 AM to 5:00

PM, and the entry fee is around 700 pesos. It's a must-do for nature enthusiasts.

Xcaret Park: Just south of Playa del Carmen, this eco-archaeological park offers a variety of activities, including underground rivers, caves, a botanical garden, and cultural performances. It's open daily from 8:00 AM to 6:00 PM, and the entry fee is around 700 pesos. It's a fantastic way to experience the natural beauty and cultural heritage of the region.

Coco Bongo: For a night of entertainment, head to Coco Bongo, a popular nightclub in the Hotel Zone. It's open from 9:00 PM to 3:00 AM, and there's a cover charge of around 400 pesos. The club features live music, DJs, and acrobatic performances.

Beach Clubs: Playa del Carmen has several beach clubs where you can relax and enjoy the day. Popular options include Mamita's Beach Club, Lido Beach Club, and Kool Beach Club.

These clubs offer lounge chairs, day beds, and food and drink options. Prices vary, but a day pass typically costs around 500 pesos.

Isla Mujeres: Just a short ferry ride from Playa del Carmen, Isla Mujeres is a charming island known for its beautiful beaches and laid-back atmosphere. You can take a day trip to explore the island, visit the turtle sanctuary, and enjoy a relaxing day by the sea.

Scuba Diving and Snorkeling: Playa del Carmen is a great spot for underwater adventures. You can go scuba diving or snorkeling to explore the vibrant marine life and coral reefs. Several dive shops offer guided tours and equipment rentals.

Local Food Tours: To get a taste of the local cuisine, consider joining a food tour. These tours take you to various eateries and street vendors, where you can sample traditional dishes like tacos, ceviche, and fresh seafood. It's a great way to experience the flavors of the region.

Temazcal Ceremony: For a unique cultural experience, you can participate in a traditional Temazcal ceremony. This is a sweat lodge ritual that involves a steam bath and herbal treatments. It's a great way to relax and connect with the local culture.

Playa del Carmen offers a mix of relaxation, adventure, and cultural experiences. Whether you're lounging on the beach, exploring underground rivers, or enjoying the vibrant nightlife, there's something for everyone in this tropical paradise. Enjoy your time in Playa del Carmen!

Tulum

Tulum is a captivating destination on the Yucatan Peninsula, blending stunning beaches, ancient Mayan ruins, and a laid-back bohemian vibe. Here's a guide to some of the top attractions and essential information to make the most of your visit.

Tulum Ruins: The iconic Tulum archaeological site is perched on a cliff overlooking the turquoise Caribbean Sea. This ancient Mayan city was a significant trading port. The site is open daily from 8:00 AM to 5:00 PM, and the entrance fee is around 80 pesos. The Castillo, the Temple of the Frescoes, and the House of the Columns are some of the main structures you'll want to explore. Don't forget your camera for those breathtaking views!

Tulum Beach: Just a short distance from the ruins, Tulum Beach boasts pristine white sand and clear blue waters. It's a great spot for sunbathing, swimming, and snorkeling. The beach is public and accessible at all times, but some sections are lined with beach clubs that offer amenities for a fee.

Gran Cenote: One of the most popular cenotes near Tulum, Gran Cenote offers crystal-clear waters perfect for swimming, snorkeling, and diving. The cenote is open daily from 8:00 AM to 5:00 PM, and the entrance fee is around 180 pesos. It's an ideal place to cool off and marvel at the underwater formations.

Cenote Dos Ojos: Located about 22 kilometers north of Tulum, Cenote Dos Ojos is famous for its extensive underwater cave system. The cenote is open daily from 8:00 AM to 5:00 PM, and the entrance fee is around 350 pesos. Whether you're snorkeling or diving, the experience here is like no other.

Tulum National Park: This protected area surrounding the Tulum ruins offers scenic walking trails through lush vegetation and along the coastline. The park is open daily from 8:00 AM to 5:00 PM, and entry is included with the ruins' entrance fee. It's a peaceful place to enjoy the natural beauty of the region.

Sian Ka'an Biosphere Reserve: A UNESCO World Heritage site, Sian Ka'an is a haven for wildlife and offers diverse ecosystems, from wetlands and mangroves to tropical forests. Tours are available, including boat trips and bird-watching excursions. The reserve is open daily from 9:00 AM to 5:00 PM, and fees vary depending on the tour.

Pablo Escobar's Casa Malca: This former mansion of the infamous drug lord is now a luxurious hotel and art gallery. Even if you're not staying there, you can visit the restaurant and explore the intriguing art installations. The gallery and restaurant are open to visitors daily from 10:00 AM to 7:00 PM.

Tulum Pueblo: The town of Tulum, known as Tulum Pueblo, is a great place to experience local culture. You'll find a variety of restaurants, shops, and markets. Don't miss the street food stalls offering delicious tacos and empanadas. The town is lively, especially in the evenings.

Yaan Wellness Energy Spa: If you're looking to relax and rejuvenate, visit Yaan Wellness Energy Spa. They offer a range of holistic treatments, including massages, temazcal ceremonies, and yoga classes. The spa is open daily from 9:00 AM to 7:00 PM.

Papaya Playa Project: This eco-friendly beach club and hotel hosts regular events, including full moon parties, live music, and wellness workshops. Even if you're not staying there, you can enjoy the beach club's amenities for a day fee. It's a great spot to unwind and socialize.

Cenote Calavera: Also known as the Temple of Doom, this cenote is a bit more off the beaten path but well worth the visit. With its three jumping points into the crystal-clear water, it's a favorite among adventurous travelers. It's open daily from 9:00 AM to 5:00 PM, and the entrance fee is around 100 pesos.

Campeche

Campeche, a charming city on the west coast of the Yucatan Peninsula, is a UNESCO World Heritage Site known for its well-preserved colonial architecture and rich history. Let's explore some of the top attractions and what you need to know about each one.

Historic Center: The heart of Campeche is its historic center, enclosed by 16th-century fortress walls. Strolling through the narrow streets, you'll find colorful buildings, charming plazas, and lively markets. The center is pedestrian-friendly, making it perfect for leisurely walks. Don't miss the Cathedral of Santa Isabel, a stunning example of baroque architecture.

Malecón de Campeche: This scenic boardwalk runs along the coastline and offers beautiful views of the sea. It's a great place to take a relaxing walk, enjoy the sunset, and watch the local fishermen at work. The Malecón is open to the public at all times and is free to visit.

Museo de la Ciudad: Located in the historic center, this museum provides a fascinating insight into the history and culture of Campeche. It's open Tuesday to Sunday from 9:00 AM to 6:00 PM, and the entry fee is around 50 pesos. The museum features exhibits on the city's colonial past, pirate attacks, and the Mayan civilization.

Zona Arquelogica Edzna: About 90 kilometers from Campeche, Edzna is an impressive Mayan archaeological site. The site is open daily from 8:00 AM to 5:00 PM, and the entry fee is around 70 pesos. You can explore the main plaza, the Temple of the Niches, and the Ball Court. It's a great day trip to experience the ancient Mayan culture.

Fuerte San Miguel: This historic fort is one of the main attractions in Campeche. It offers a glimpse into the city's defensive history and provides stunning views of the surrounding area. The fort is open daily from 9:00 AM to 6:00 PM, and the entry fee is around 40 pesos.

Casa No. 6: This cultural center is housed in a beautifully restored colonial building. It hosts art exhibitions, workshops, and cultural events. The center is open Tuesday to Sunday from 10:00 AM to 6:00 PM, and the entry fee is around 50 pesos. It's a great place to immerse yourself in the local arts scene.

Calakmul: Located in the Calakmul Biosphere Reserve, this ancient Mayan city is one of the largest and most important archaeological sites in Mexico. The site is open daily from 8:00 AM to 5:00 PM, and the entry fee is around 70 pesos. It's a bit of a journey from Campeche, but it's well worth it for history enthusiasts.

Isla Aguada: This small island is a short boat ride from Campeche and offers a peaceful escape from the city. The island has a beautiful beach, a lighthouse, and a small restaurant. It's a great spot for a day trip to relax and enjoy the natural beauty.

Hacienda Uayamon: This historic hacienda is located about 40 kilometers from Campeche and offers a glimpse into the region's agricultural past. The hacienda is open daily from 9:00 AM to 5:00 PM, and the entry fee is around 50 pesos. You can explore the main house, the chapel, and the surrounding gardens.

Poésia del Mar: This magical fountain show is a popular attraction in Campeche. Located in the historic center, the show features colorful water displays set to music. It's a fun and enchanting experience for all ages.

Valladolid

Valladolid, a picturesque city in the heart of Spain's Castile and León region, is steeped in history and culture. Let's explore some of the top attractions and what you need to know about each one.

Plaza Mayor de Valladolid: This charming square is the heart of the city, surrounded by historic buildings and bustling cafes. It's a great place to relax, people-watch, and soak in the local atmosphere. The square is open to the public at all times and is free to visit.

Museo Nacional de Escultura: Housed in the former Colegio de San Gregorio, this museum boasts an impressive collection of sculptures from the late Middle Ages to the Baroque period. The museum is open Tuesday to Sunday from 9:00 AM to 6:00 PM, and the entry fee is around 5 euros. It's a must-visit for art enthusiasts.

Iglesia de San Pablo: This stunning church is known for its intricately carved facade, a masterpiece of Isabelline Gothic style. The church is open daily from 10:00 AM to 6:00 PM, and there's no entry fee. It's a beautiful example of medieval architecture.

Casa-Museo de Colón: This museum is dedicated to Christopher Columbus and his connection to Valladolid. It features interactive exhibits and historical artifacts. The museum is open Tuesday to Sunday from 10:00 AM to 6:00 PM, and the entry fee is around 4 euros. It's a fascinating place to learn about the explorer's life and legacy.

Casa de Cervantes: This house was once the residence of the famous writer Miguel de Cervantes. It's now a museum showcasing period furnishings and exhibits about his life. The museum is open Tuesday to Sunday from 10:00 AM to 6:00 PM, and the entry fee is around 3 euros. It's a great spot for literature lovers.

Palacio de Pimentel: This historic palace is where King Felipe II was born. It's open to the public on weekends from 10:00 AM to 6:00 PM, and the entry fee is around 3 euros. The palace features beautiful architecture and a tiled mural depicting scenes from the king's life.

Catedral de Valladolid: This 16th-century cathedral is known for its extravagant altarpiece and processional monstrance. The cathedral is open daily from 10:00 AM to 6:00 PM, and there's no entry fee. It's a stunning example of Spanish religious architecture.

Plaza de San Pablo: This open square is dominated by the exquisite Iglesia de San Pablo. It's a lovely spot to sit and enjoy the surroundings. The square is open to the public at all times and is free to visit.

Museo Patio Herreriano: This museum is dedicated to post-WWI Spanish art and features works by Salvador Dalí, Joan Miró, and Eduardo Chillida. The museum is open Tuesday to

Sunday from 10:00 AM to 6:00 PM, and the entry fee is around 5 euros. It's a great place to explore modern Spanish art.

Ruins of the Collegiate Church: These 13th-century ruins are located atop the northeastern perimeter of the cathedral. They offer a glimpse into the city's medieval past. The ruins are open daily from 10:00 AM to 6:00 PM, and there's no entry fee.

Iglesia de Santa María la Antigua: This pretty Gothic church features an elegant Romanesque tower. The church is open daily from 10:00 AM to 6:00 PM, and there's no entry fee. It's a peaceful place to admire the architecture.

Chetumal

Chetumal, the capital of Quintana Roo state in Mexico, is a vibrant city located on the east coast of the Yucatan Peninsula, near the Belize border. Here are some highlights and things to know about Chetumal:

Historic Significance: Chetumal has a rich history, originally founded as a Mayan settlement. The city was officially established as a Mexican port town in 1898, originally named Payo Obispo. It became the capital of Quintana Roo in 1974.

Museo de la Cultura Maya: This interactive museum offers fascinating insights into the Mayan civilization. It's a great place to learn about the region's history and culture.

Malecón de Chetumal: This scenic boardwalk along the coastline is perfect for a relaxing walk, enjoying the sea breeze, and watching local fishermen at work.

Zona Arqueológica de Dzibanché - Kinichná: This archaeological site features ancient ruins and offers a glimpse into the region's pre-Columbian past.

Cenote Tajma Ha: A beautiful cenote near Chetumal, ideal for swimming and exploring underwater caves.

Chetumal Bay: The bay offers opportunities for fishing, boating, and enjoying the coastal scenery.

Local Cuisine: Chetumal has a variety of restaurants serving delicious local dishes, including seafood and traditional Mexican cuisine.

Climate: Chetumal has a tropical climate, so be prepared for warm weather and occasional rain.

Transportation: The city has a commercial airport, Chetumal International Airport, and is well-connected by road to other major cities in the region.

Progreso

Progreso, a charming port city on the Yucatan Peninsula, is known for its beautiful beaches, rich history, and vibrant culture. Here are some highlights and things to know about Progreso:

Progreso Pier is famous for being the world's longest pier, stretching about 6.5 kilometers (4 miles) into the Gulf of Mexico. It's a popular spot for fishing, strolling, and enjoying the sea breeze.

The city offers lovely white-sand beaches where you can relax, swim, and soak up the sun. Playa Progreso is a favorite among locals and visitors alike.

Progreso has a rich cultural heritage, with influences from the Mayan civilization and Spanish colonial history. You can explore local markets, enjoy traditional Mexican cuisine, and visit historical sites.

The city is a frequent stop for cruise ships, making it a gateway for tourists to explore the Yucatan Peninsula. The pier allows passengers to disembark directly onto the beach.

Progreso is conveniently located near major Mayan archaeological sites like Uxmal and Dzibilchaltun, making it an ideal base for exploring the region's history.

The city has a tropical climate with warm temperatures year-round. The best time to visit is during the dry season from December to April.

Don't miss trying the local seafood and traditional dishes at the various restaurants and street vendors in Progreso.

Progreso is well-connected by road to other major cities in the region, including Merida, which is about a 30-minute drive away.

Isla Mujeres

Isla Mujeres, a beautiful island off the coast of the Yucatan Peninsula, is a tropical paradise known for its stunning beaches, vibrant marine life, and relaxed atmosphere. Here are some highlights and things to know about Isla Mujeres:

Playa Norte: This beach is famous for its soft, white sand and clear turquoise waters. It's a perfect spot for sunbathing, swimming, and snorkeling.

Punta Sur: Located at the southern tip of the island, this area features a lighthouse and a turtle sanctuary. It's a great place for hiking and enjoying panoramic views of the island.

Isla Mujeres Museum: This museum offers a fascinating look into the island's history and culture, with exhibits on the Mayan civilization and the island's maritime heritage.

El Centro: The main town on the island, El Centro, is filled with charming shops, restaurants, and cafes. It's a great place to explore and experience the local culture.

Isla Mujeres Aquarium: An interactive aquarium where you can see a variety of marine life, including sharks, rays, and tropical fish. It's a fun and educational experience for all ages.

Isla Contoy: A nearby island that can be visited on a day trip. It's a protected area and a haven for birdwatchers and nature enthusiasts.

Local Cuisine: Don't miss trying the fresh seafood and traditional Mexican dishes at the various restaurants and street vendors on the island.

Activities: Isla Mujeres offers a range of activities, including snorkeling, diving, kayaking, and boat tours. You can also rent mopeds to explore the island at your own pace.

Climate: The island has a tropical climate with warm temperatures year-round. The best time to visit is during the dry season from December to April.

Transportation: You can reach Isla Mujeres by ferry from Cancun or Playa del Carmen. The island is small enough to explore on foot or by moped.

Bacalar

Bacalar, a hidden gem in the southern part of Quintana Roo, Mexico, is known for its stunning freshwater lagoon, Laguna Bacalar, also called "La Laguna de los Siete Colores" (The Lagoon of Seven Colors). Here are some highlights and things to know about Bacalar:

Laguna Bacalar is mesmerizing, famous for its gradient blues, which create a stunning visual effect. It's a popular spot for kayaking, canoeing, and boat tours.

Fuerte San Felipe Bacalar is a historic fort completed in 1729 to protect the town from pirates. Visitors can explore the fortress and learn about its history.

Cocalitos is a beautiful area perfect for swimming and enjoying the natural beauty of the lagoon.

Adventure Hub: Bacalar is quickly becoming an adventure destination, offering activities like snorkeling, diving, and exploring nearby archaeological sites like Limones and Chacchoben.

Pueblo Mágico: Bacalar was designated as one of Mexico's "Pueblos Mágicos" in 2006, recognizing its architectural, historical, and cultural importance.

Climate: Bacalar has a tropical climate with warm temperatures year-round. The best time to visit is during the dry season from December to April.

Local Cuisine: Enjoy fresh seafood and traditional Mexican dishes at the various restaurants and street vendors in Bacalar.

Getting There: Bacalar is about an hour north of the Belize border and around 4 hours south of Cancun. It's well-connected by road and is also served by the Tren Maya.

Cultural Experiences

Mayan Traditions and Practices

Mayan traditions and practices have shaped the culture and history of the Yucatán Peninsula for centuries. The ancient Maya left behind a legacy of intricate rituals, sophisticated architecture, and deep spiritual beliefs that continue to influence the region today.

The Maya had a profound connection with the natural world, and this is evident in many of their practices. One of the most significant aspects of Mayan tradition is their calendar system. The Maya used a complex calendar that included the Tzolk'in (sacred calendar) and the Haab' (solar calendar). These calendars were used not just to mark the passage of time, but to plan agricultural activities, religious ceremonies, and political events. Today, you can still see the remnants of this timekeeping in the region's festivals and agricultural practices.

Mayan ceremonies often involved offerings to the gods. These could include food, drink, and even bloodletting rituals. The Maya believed that blood was a powerful offering that could appease the gods and ensure the community's prosperity. While these practices have largely faded, the spiritual connection to the earth remains. Many modern Maya continue to hold ceremonies that honor the natural elements, asking for rain, good harvests, or protection.

One of the most fascinating aspects of Mayan culture is their use of cenotes for rituals. Cenotes are natural sinkholes filled with water, and they were considered sacred entrances to the underworld. The Maya would make offerings to the gods by throwing valuable items, and sometimes even human sacrifices, into these cenotes. Today, these sites are popular tourist attractions, and you can still feel the sense of reverence and mystery when visiting them.

Mayan language and glyphs also hold a significant place in their tradition. The intricate hieroglyphic writing system was used to record historical events, royal lineages, and religious texts. Efforts to decipher these glyphs have provided valuable insights into Mayan society. In modern times, there are initiatives to preserve and teach the Mayan language, ensuring that this rich cultural heritage is not lost.

Mayan architecture is another enduring legacy. The great pyramids and temples, such as those at Chichén Itzá, Uxmal, and Tulum, showcase their advanced engineering skills and astronomical knowledge. These structures were often aligned with celestial events, demonstrating the Maya's sophisticated understanding of astronomy. Visiting these sites offers a glimpse into the grandeur of ancient Mayan civilization and their deep connection to the cosmos.

Traditional Mayan clothing and textiles are still woven and worn by many Maya today. The colorful patterns and intricate designs often have symbolic meanings and are made using traditional methods passed down through generations. Markets in Yucatán are a great place to see and purchase these beautiful textiles, supporting local artisans and preserving these ancient techniques.

Mayan cuisine also reflects their deep connection to the land. Staples like maize, beans, and squash were central to their diet and remain important in modern Yucatán cuisine. Traditional dishes like tamales, pibil (slow-cooked pork), and atole (a maize-based beverage) are still enjoyed today, offering a taste of the past.

The modern Maya continue to celebrate their heritage through festivals and dances. Events like the Hanal Pixan (Day of the Dead) blend ancient practices with Catholic traditions, creating a unique cultural expression. These celebrations are a vibrant and colorful reminder of the enduring Mayan spirit.

Local Handicrafts and Artisans

Exploring local handicrafts and meeting artisans in the Yucatán Peninsula is like stepping into a vibrant tapestry of culture and tradition. These crafts reflect the deep-rooted history and artistic ingenuity of the region, offering a fascinating glimpse into its heritage.

Start your journey in Mérida, where the bustling markets and quaint shops are filled with colorful textiles, intricate embroidery, and handcrafted jewelry. The city is renowned for its hammocks, made using techniques passed down through generations. Visiting a local artisan's workshop, you'll see how these hammocks are meticulously woven, creating pieces that are both functional and beautiful. The soft, breathable fabric makes them perfect for the region's warm climate.

Head to the small towns around Valladolid, where you can find traditional huipils—embroidered tunics worn by Mayan women. These garments are often adorned with vibrant patterns that carry symbolic meanings, representing everything from nature to ancestral stories. Each huipil is a labor of love, taking weeks or even months to complete. The town of Tixkokob is particularly famous for its hammocks and textiles.

In Izamal, known as the "Yellow City" for its golden-hued buildings, you'll find artisans creating stunning jewelry from silver and gold. The intricate designs often incorporate traditional Mayan motifs, blending ancient and modern styles. This town is also a great place to find handmade ceramics and pottery, crafted using techniques that date back centuries. The pieces are often decorated with bright, bold colors that echo the vibrancy of the local culture.

Uxmal and the surrounding areas offer unique crafts inspired by ancient Mayan art and architecture. Stone carvers create detailed replicas of Mayan glyphs and sculptures, while woodworkers produce beautiful items ranging from small figurines to large furniture pieces. These crafts make for meaningful souvenirs that carry a piece of the region's history.

If you're in Cancún or Playa del Carmen, don't miss the chance to visit local markets and shops selling handmade leather goods. Artisans here produce a variety of items, including bags, belts, and sandals, all crafted with a keen eye for detail and quality. The leather is often sourced locally, ensuring that each piece is authentically Yucatecan.

Throughout the Yucatán Peninsula, you'll also find beautiful baskets and mats made from henequen, a type of agave plant. This plant was once the backbone of the region's economy, and its fibers are still used today to create durable and attractive items. The craftsmanship involved in weaving these fibers into intricate patterns is truly remarkable.

Cozumel and Isla Mujeres are excellent places to discover unique marine-inspired crafts. Here, artisans use materials like shells, coral, and mother-of-pearl to create stunning jewelry and decorative items. The island's natural beauty is reflected in each piece, making them perfect mementos of your visit.

When exploring the region's markets and workshops, don't hesitate to strike up a conversation with the artisans. They often have fascinating stories to tell about their craft and the history behind it. Buying directly from these skilled creators not only supports their livelihoods but also helps preserve the rich cultural heritage of the Yucatán Peninsula.

Engaging with local handicrafts and artisans in the Yucatán Peninsula is more than just shopping; it's an enriching experience that connects you with the heart and soul of this captivating region. From intricately woven textiles to beautifully crafted jewelry, each piece tells a story of tradition, creativity, and cultural pride.

Music and Dance

The Yucatán Peninsula resonates with the rich rhythms and vibrant dances of its cultural heritage. Music and dance are integral parts of life here, weaving stories of history, celebration, and tradition.

One of the most prominent musical styles in the region is Jarana, a genre that blends Spanish and indigenous influences. The lively, upbeat tunes are typically played on instruments like the guitar, trumpet, and drums. Jarana music often

137

accompanies traditional dances during local festivals and celebrations. The dancers, dressed in colorful, embroidered garments known as huipils for women and guayaberas for men, move with graceful yet energetic steps, creating a mesmerizing performance.

Another key aspect of Yucatán's musical landscape is Trova Yucateca. This genre of romantic, melodic songs is akin to the troubadour tradition. Trova music often features the guitar and the requinto, a smaller, higher-pitched guitar, and the lyrics are poetic and soulful. Serenades, where singers perform romantic songs under the windows of loved ones, are a beloved tradition in many towns.

Danza de los Parachicos is a vibrant dance performed during the annual Fiesta Grande in Chiapa de Corzo. Dancers don colorful costumes and masks, moving rhythmically to the music of marimbas, drums, and flutes. This dance has been declared a UNESCO Intangible Cultural Heritage, showcasing the region's rich folkloric traditions.

The sound of the marimba, a percussion instrument of wooden bars, is also common in the Yucatán Peninsula. It's an essential part of many local celebrations and festivals, producing a melodic, rhythmic sound that encourages dancing and festivity.

In addition to these traditional forms, contemporary music also thrives in the Yucatán. Local bands and musicians often blend traditional sounds with modern genres like rock, jazz, and pop, creating unique and innovative music that appeals to both locals and visitors.

Dance is equally important in the cultural fabric of the region. The Danzón, a dance that originated in Cuba but has become a staple in Mexican culture, is popular in the Yucatán. Couples glide elegantly across the dance floor, often in public squares during evening events. The dance is characterized by its slow, rhythmic movements and close embrace.

Salsa and merengue are also widely enjoyed, with many clubs and venues offering live music and dance lessons. These energetic dances are a great way to experience the local nightlife and connect with the vibrant spirit of the people.

Festivals and public performances are an excellent way to experience the music and dance of the Yucatán Peninsula. During Carnaval, held in the weeks leading up to Lent, towns and cities come alive with parades, music, and dancing. The streets are filled with revelers in colorful costumes, and the air is filled with the sounds of traditional and contemporary music.

In Mérida, the weekly Noche Mexicana and Vaquería events offer free public performances of traditional music and dance. These events are held in the city's main square and are a fantastic way to immerse yourself in the local culture.

Music and dance in the Yucatán Peninsula are not just art forms; they are expressions of community and identity. They tell the stories of the past, celebrate the present, and inspire the future. Whether you're listening to the romantic strains of Trova, dancing to the lively rhythms of Jarana, or enjoying the melodic sounds of the marimba, the music and dance of the Yucatán will undoubtedly leave a lasting impression on your heart.

Festivals and Celebrations

The Yucatán Peninsula is a vibrant tapestry of festivals and celebrations, each offering a unique glimpse into the region's rich cultural heritage. These events are marked by colorful parades, traditional music and dance, and a deep sense of community and tradition.

One of the most significant celebrations is Hanal Pixán, the Mayan Day of the Dead. Held from October 31 to November 2, this festival honors deceased loved ones with offerings of food, flowers, and candles. Families build altars in their homes and visit cemeteries to decorate graves and share stories of the departed. The air is filled with the aroma of traditional foods like pib, a special tamale cooked in an underground oven. The atmosphere is one of reverence and celebration, a beautiful blend of Mayan and Catholic traditions.

Carnaval is another major event, taking place in the week leading up to Lent. Cities like Mérida, Progreso, and Cozumel come alive with parades, music, dancing, and elaborate costumes. The streets are filled with revelers enjoying the festive atmosphere. Each city has its own unique twist on the celebration, but all share a common spirit of joy and community.

Fiesta de la Candelaria, celebrated in early February in the town of Valladolid, is a religious and cultural festival honoring the Virgin of Candelaria. The event includes processions, traditional dances, music, and a livestock fair. The town square is filled with vendors selling crafts, food, and souvenirs, creating a lively and colorful scene.

In March, the Spring Equinox at Chichén Itzá draws thousands of visitors to witness the incredible sight of the "serpent" descending the steps of El Castillo, the main pyramid. This phenomenon occurs when the sun casts a series of shadows that resemble a snake slithering down the pyramid's side. The event is accompanied by music, dances, and ceremonies celebrating the Mayan culture.

Grito de Dolores on September 15 is the Mexican Independence Day celebration. In every town and city across the Yucatán, people gather in public squares to listen to the reenactment of Miguel Hidalgo's historic call for independence. The night is filled with fireworks, music, and street parties, creating an electric atmosphere of national pride and joy.

Noche Blanca in Mérida is a cultural festival held twice a year, in May and December. The city's museums, galleries, and cultural centers stay open late, offering free admission and special events. The streets are filled with live music, art installations, performances, and food stalls, making it a night of cultural immersion and community celebration.

In November, Festival de Vida y Muerte at Xcaret Park is a unique celebration of the Day of the Dead. The park transforms into a vibrant display of altars, performances, and traditional foods. Visitors can enjoy concerts, theater, dance, and workshops that showcase the rich traditions of the holiday.

Throughout the year, smaller towns and villages host their own patron saint festivals, known as fiestas patronales. These celebrations often include religious processions, rodeos, traditional dances, and communal meals. Each town has its own unique customs and traditions, offering a glimpse into the local culture and way of life.

Whether you're witnessing the mystical equinox at Chichén Itzá, dancing in the streets during Carnaval, or experiencing the poignant beauty of Hanal Pixán, the festivals and celebrations of the Yucatán Peninsula provide a rich and immersive cultural experience. They are a testament to the region's deep-rooted traditions, communal spirit, and vibrant cultural life.

Engaging with Local Communities

Engaging with local communities in the Yucatán Peninsula offers a deeply enriching experience that goes beyond the typical tourist attractions. It allows you to connect with the culture, traditions, and people in a meaningful way. Here's how you can dive into the local lifestyle:

First, consider staying in locally-owned accommodations rather than large, international hotels. Boutique hotels, guesthouses, and homestays offer a more personal touch and often provide insights into local customs and traditions. Plus, your stay helps support the local economy directly. In towns like Valladolid, you might find charming colonial homes converted into cozy bed-and-breakfasts, where hosts share stories about the area's history and daily life.

Participating in community tours is another fantastic way to engage. Many local guides offer tours that delve into the region's cultural heritage, natural beauty, and daily life. For example, you can join a guided tour to explore traditional Mayan villages where you'll see firsthand how locals live and work. You might learn about traditional farming practices, see how tortillas are made from scratch, or participate in a Mayan purification ceremony.

Visiting local markets is a must. Markets like Mercado Lucas de Gálvez in Mérida or the markets in smaller towns are bustling hubs of activity. Here, you can buy fresh produce, handmade crafts, and traditional foods. Take the time to chat with vendors – they're often more than willing to share stories about their goods and the cultural significance behind them. Try to pick up some basic Spanish phrases; even simple greetings can go a long way in building rapport.

Volunteering is a rewarding way to give back to the community while gaining a deeper understanding of local life. There are various opportunities available, from teaching English or participating in environmental conservation projects to helping out at local community centers. Organizations like Amigos de

Sian Ka'an offer volunteer programs focused on preserving the region's unique ecosystems.

Attending local festivals and events is a wonderful way to experience the Yucatán's vibrant culture. Whether it's a religious festival, a traditional dance performance, or a local fair, these events provide a window into the community's heart and soul. Engage with locals, join in the dances, and taste the traditional foods – it's an immersive experience that you'll remember long after your trip.

Workshops and classes are also great for connecting with the culture. Many local artisans offer workshops where you can learn traditional crafts like pottery, weaving, or hammock making. These hands-on experiences not only teach you new skills but also provide a deeper appreciation for the artistry and effort behind these beautiful items.

Supporting local businesses is crucial. Whether it's dining at a family-run restaurant, purchasing souvenirs from local artisans, or booking tours through local companies, your choices can have a positive impact on the community. Dining at local eateries gives you a chance to savor authentic Yucatecan cuisine and perhaps even learn the stories behind the dishes.

Lastly, always approach these interactions with respect and openness. Be mindful of cultural differences and show appreciation for the hospitality you receive. Engaging with local communities in a meaningful way enriches your travel experience and fosters a deeper connection with the Yucatán Peninsula. It turns your visit into an exchange of cultures, where both visitors and locals can learn and benefit from each other.

Planning Your Trip

ACCOMMODATION

Luxury Accommodation

Features: High-end furnishings, private balconies, spa and wellness facilities, gourmet dining options, personalized services.

Offers: Complimentary breakfast, room upgrades, late check-out, exclusive access to amenities.

Estimated Price: $300+ per night.

Nearness to Attractions: Typically located in prime areas, close to major attractions.

Suitability: Ideal for solo travelers seeking a luxurious and pampered experience.

Midrange Accommodation

Features: Comfortable rooms with private bathrooms, air conditioning, television, fitness centers, swimming pools.

Offers: Free Wi-Fi, breakfast included, shuttle services, discounts on local attractions.

Estimated Price: $150-$300 per night.

Nearness to Attractions: Conveniently located, often within walking distance to popular sites.

Suitability: Suitable for solo travelers looking for comfort and convenience at a moderate price.

Budget Accommodation

Features: Basic rooms with essential amenities like a bed, clean linens, shared bathroom facilities.

Offers: Dormitory-style rooms, communal kitchens, free Wi-Fi, social events.

Estimated Price: $50-$150 per night.

Nearness to Attractions: Often located in central city areas or near public transportation.

Suitability: Great for solo travelers on a tight budget who want to meet other travelers and save on costs.

Packing Essentials

When preparing for a trip, it's important to pack smart to ensure you have everything you need without overpacking. Here's a comprehensive list of packing essentials to help you get ready for your adventure:

Clothing:

- Lightweight and breathable clothing for warm weather
- A light jacket or sweater for cooler evenings
- Comfortable walking shoes or sandals
- Swimwear if you plan to hit the beach or pool
- A hat or cap for sun protection
- Sunglasses
- Undergarments and socks
- Pajamas

Toiletries:
- Toothbrush and toothpaste
- Shampoo and conditioner (travel-sized)
- Body wash or soap
- Deodorant
- Razor and shaving cream
- Hairbrush or comb
- Sunscreen with high SPF

- Insect repellent

- Travel-sized first aid kit (band-aids, antiseptic wipes, pain relievers)

Health and Safety:

- Any prescription medications, with copies of the prescription

- Hand sanitizer and disinfectant wipes

- Face masks

- Travel insurance documents

Electronics:

- Mobile phone and charger

- Power bank for extra battery life

- Camera and memory cards

- Travel adapter if needed

- Headphones or earbuds

- Laptop or tablet (if you need to stay connected)

Documents:

- Passport and copies of your passport

- ID card or driver's license

- Printed copies of flight and accommodation confirmations

- Emergency contact information

- Credit cards and some cash in local currency

Other Essentials:

- Reusable water bottle

- Snacks for the journey

- A good book or e-reader for entertainment

- Travel pillow and eye mask for long flights

- A small daypack or backpack for day trips

Useful Phrases and Language Tips

When traveling to a new place, it's always helpful to know a few local phrases and tips to make communication smoother and your experience more enjoyable. Here are some useful phrases and language tips for Spanish, which is widely spoken across the Yucatán Peninsula and other parts of Mexico.

Basic Phrases:

- Hello: Hola

- Good morning: Buenos días

- Good afternoon: Buenas tardes

- Good evening: Buenas noches

- Goodbye: Adiós

- Please: Por favor

- Thank you: Gracias

- You're welcome: De nada

- Yes: Sí

- No: No

- Excuse me: Perdón or Disculpa

- I'm sorry: Lo siento

- Do you speak English?: ¿Hablas inglés?

- I don't understand: No entiendo

- Could you repeat that, please?: ¿Podrías repetir eso, por favor?

- Where is…?: ¿Dónde está…?

- How much does it cost?: ¿Cuánto cuesta?

- What time is it?: ¿Qué hora es?

- My name is…: Me llamo…

- Nice to meet you: Mucho gusto

Dining and Shopping:

- A table for one, please: Una mesa para uno, por favor

- Can I see the menu?: ¿Puedo ver el menú?

- I would like…: Me gustaría…

- The check, please: La cuenta, por favor

- Do you accept credit cards?: ¿Aceptan tarjetas de crédito?

- Can I have a bag?: ¿Puedo tener una bolsa?

- I'm just looking: Solo estoy mirando

Directions and Transportation:

- Where is the bathroom?: ¿Dónde está el baño?

- How do I get to…?: ¿Cómo llego a…?

- Is it far?: ¿Está lejos?

- Turn right/left: Gira a la derecha/izquierda

- Straight ahead: Todo recto

- How much is the fare?: ¿Cuánto es la tarifa?

- I need a taxi: Necesito un taxi

Tips:

- Pronunciation: Spanish pronunciation is relatively consistent, but pay attention to rolling your "r"s and pronouncing vowels clearly.

- Politeness: Using "please" (por favor) and "thank you" (gracias) is very important in Spanish-speaking cultures.

- Gestures: Non-verbal communication like smiles, nods, and hand gestures can also help convey your meaning.

- Context: Understanding context is key. Words can have different meanings in different situations, so listening carefully can help you understand better.

- Practice: Don't be afraid to practice. Locals appreciate when visitors make an effort to speak their language, even if it's just a few words.

Conclusion

As you close this travel guide, we hope you feel well-prepared and inspired to explore the Yucatán Peninsula, a region where history, culture, and natural beauty converge in unforgettable ways. From the ancient ruins of the Maya to the vibrant festivals that bring the streets to life, the Yucatán offers an endless array of experiences waiting to be discovered.

Whether you're lounging on pristine beaches, swimming in mystical cenotes, or savoring the rich flavors of Yucatecan cuisine, each moment in this enchanting region is an opportunity to connect with its deep-rooted traditions and warm-hearted people. The adventures you'll embark upon and the memories you'll create will not only enrich your understanding of this unique part of the world but also leave an indelible mark on your heart.

As you journey through the Yucatán Peninsula, remember to immerse yourself in its local communities, respect its cultural heritage, and cherish the natural wonders that make this place so special. Your travels here will be more than a series of destinations—they will be a collection of stories, encounters, and experiences that shape your perspective and deepen your appreciation for the world.